HISTORY
5 to 9

Joan Blyth

HODDER AND STOUGHTON
LONDON SYDNEY AUCKLAND TORONTO

To my son, Richard,
who first aroused my interest in young children.

Many of the references in this book are derived from a
piece of research which was carried out while I was a
non-stipendiary Research Fellow, at the Froebel
Educational Institute, from 1983 to 1985

ISBN 0 340 40426 4
First published 1988
Second impression 1989
Copyright © 1988 Joan Blyth

Printed and bound in Great Britain for
Hodder and Stoughton Educational,
a division of Hodder and Stoughton Ltd,
Mill Road, Dunton Green, Sevenoaks, Kent,
by The Eastern Press Ltd, Reading.

Typeset by Wessex Typesetters
(Division of The Eastern Press Ltd)
Frome, Somerset

Contents

1 Children's need for the past

History remains the one discipline in the curriculum that is concerned with the behaviour of human beings.[1]

In first schools, the subject is now virtually non-existent. The most clear-cut evidence of this trend can be seen in the absence from many headteachers' time-tables of schemes of work, as from many teachers' lesson plans, of any reference to history in its own right, or indeed, in any form.[2]

Here are two views expressed by well-known administrators in education at the time of the 1978 Primary Survey from the Department of Education and Science.[3] The first may be challenged by some educationalists but has much truth in it. They are both published in the same journal, the mouthpiece of the DES, yet they appear to contradict each other. If history is an essential element of the curriculum because of its intrinsic involvement with humanity, why is it 'non-existent' in first schools? There has not been much improvement in the last nine years, though the last two or three years have seen an upsurge of interest in the early years generally. This may be on account of the greater numbers in the 4 to 9 age range in the schools and the greater emphasis on specialisms in the primary years. To some, the purpose of specialisation is to raise academic standards all round and give a more satisfactory diet to abler children.

This consensus of opinion by those in authority is not translated into action for many reasons. Foremost amongst these is the disagreement of headteachers and many teacher trainers with the teaching of history at all, particularly as far as the 5 to 9 years are concerned. Does this spring from the pressure to teach the basics and the increasing size of classes and dearth of teachers? Or is it the philosophy of the 'seamless robe' of learning, which necessitates integration and interdisciplinary studies? Coupled with this, the 1967 Plowden Report[4] and 'discovery learning' do not encourage a systematic planning of schemes and resources, essential to a study of the past.

Taking the problem a stage further in analysis, headteachers do not see the past as useful knowledge and experience, to help children survive life in a rapidly changing world. The emphasis on technical and vocational training in secondary schools and the recent suggestion of new city technology schools, supports this view and is influencing adversely the popularity of history in secondary schools. Are we better without knowledge of our own and other people's past in order to look forward with confidence? Are we not told by the Italian historian Benedetto Croce that 'We learn from history that we do not learn from history'?

Children in the 'early years' (5 to 9) have a

small past of their own to remember but they can learn from even five years of life. I believe that children *need* the past, and teachers should be helped to show them how it can be used and built upon for the future.

Too many teachers had unhappy experiences of history during their own secondary school days, unless they were blessed with encyclopaedic memories or were fortunate to encounter the rare inspired teacher of history. They therefore have little impetus to seek out interesting ways of approaching the subject with young children. Nor do they receive much encouragement from many headteachers, LEA Advisers or publishers. Many teachers have a traditional view of history as being the chronology of all countries of the world in all classes of society, perhaps with an emphasis on 'kings and things' prominent in publishers' catalogues, but complex and remote from ordinary people's lives. Teachers must decide what small part of the past to use at each stage of the four first school years. It matters little how far back the teacher goes or that the past which is taught has many gaps in it. It should be detailed study over a few years or decades and be linked to the child's experience in the first place. (More help is given in Chapter 4 on these decisions.) To children aged between 5 and 9 any part of the past, in any country, of even the shortest duration, is genuine historical study. This knowledge should encourage all primary teachers to venture into the teaching of history with the confidence that family history, oral history and local history are all as valid a form of history as the more traditional approaches of kings, wars and politics. They should remember in the words of the archaeologist Dr C. Hills, that 'the past is not another place'.

Having decided that she is capable of undertaking this area of teaching, the general primary teacher must consider why her children need the past in order to make her efforts worthwhile and to tailor them to the children's specific requirements. There seem to be three areas to bear in mind. The first is the fulfilment of personal, inward-looking needs, necessary to help the child develop as a well-adjusted, stable adult. Another is the area concerned with other people, the outward-looking needs of the child in relation to society. The third area embraces the practical needs of the child using the essential historical concepts and skills learnt in a study of the past. A sense of historic time is the greatest contribution made by history in all learning.

History fulfils the psychological inward-looking needs of children

Human nature, as it stands, makes mankind naturally self-centred and therefore selfish. The education of children at home and at school is part of the process of leading children from this inward-looking preoccupation to thinking of others and being unselfish in attitudes, word and actions. Knowing about themselves, their families and their past helps children to understand why they are as they are, for good or ill. According to Arthur Marwick, history is man's collective memory which he loses at his peril. 'As a man without memory and self-knowledge is a man adrift, so a society without a memory (or more correctly, without recollection) and self-knowledge would be a society adrift.'[5] As a philosopher-historian has written, history 'teaches us what man has done and thus what man is'[6] and for a child to know himself, 'warts and all', and what he can and cannot do, is the beginning of personal wisdom and a happy life. For example, Francis Drake was the sort of person who dared to circumnavigate the world in a small ship, *The Golden Hind*, but most of us could not contemplate this. Both the Romans and Hitler were obsessed by power and were too ambitious in their acquisition of land; they failed miserably in the end. The moral is to accept your strengths and limitations and plan your life within those. The 'behaviour of human beings' (in the words of John Slater) is unpredictable and uncertain both inside and outside the family. Children too often become victims of adults and the past can help them to be on their guard and also understand the whims of those around them. The recent pressure on children to say 'No' and not to go with strangers or succumb to the physical advances of any adults, has led to direct teaching from the past experience of society. Children have been found to be quick to learn. Similarly, children's learning of road safety and about the place of festivals in society arises from direct teaching in relation to experience.

Many adults lead unbalanced emotional lives as a result of their upbringing and are unable to experience outgoing, empathetic feelings. John Slater's description of the response of one primary headmaster, who taught his children about nineteenth-century factory children from original sources, is direct and simple. He was trying to achieve a heartfelt response from them: 'I want to make them weep.'[7] Children who can weep for other people's feelings will grow up into sympathetic adults. Thus teaching about the past can begin to overcome 'the stiff upper lip' which has caused many small boys problems in their future relationships. This sympathy can also be developed into an awareness of the overt and hidden discrimination suffered by various sections of society. More will be said in Chapter 5 about how teachers can teach the past to stimulate these feelings.

Children who understand themselves, their thoughts and weaknesses, become more confident, self-respecting adults, knowing that they have a purposeful role to fulfil in society. Too many adults have encountered problems in life as a result of a lack of confidence, and this applies particularly to the less advantaged of any colour, sex or minority group. Knowing about people in the past and discussing them with teachers and their peers helps children to have the confidence to cope with people in life. The determination of William Wilberforce to end slavery, Florence Nightingale to improve the care of the sick and Marie Curie to find a cure for cancer are examples of endurance in the cause of social betterment which can give children confidence when tackling difficult tasks. The views of psychologists on the need for attention to early emotional problems will be discussed in Chapter 3.

History fulfils the outward-looking needs of children

A child who understands himself and has confidence in his powers, however limited they may be, needs to move out from this position to try to understand the world around him. This world includes other children, his family (near and far) and his teachers. It also includes knowledge of many areas of information for an appreciation of various forms of the media. This is particularly important for the understanding of television both at home and at school. School television programmes are usually explained by the teacher and limited in duration, but television in many homes is unexplained and ever present. Young children who are victims of this social situation need particular help from school. References to South Africa, Libya, Ireland, the Arabs and the Falkland Islands are confusing to children unless they have an outline knowledge of the issues involved. Most of these issues depend upon geography but are also historically based and have a past history going back far beyond the birth of the children concerned.

Celebrations and anniversaries, which fill the media, encourage an awareness of the past through their very nature. Although Christmas is a religious festival, Christ's birth and life happened in time and the references to his work in the Bible depict the social life of the first century AD in a particular country. Similar considerations apply to the place in history of Mohammed and Guru Nanak. Royal weddings involve knowledge of family trees, traditions, customs and relationships far into the past. Resources for schools on these occasions are plentiful and usually well documented. Royal weddings can be compared; those of Prince Andrew and the Prince of Wales with those of Queen Victoria and Henry VIII, for example. (Why did Henry VIII have so many weddings?) Centenaries of

Figure 1.1 *The wedding of Prince Andrew and Sarah Ferguson*

schools have proved most successful whole-school activities linking 5 to 11 year olds. Comparison of a school in 1887 with one in 1987 is very relevant, especially if the same school is used. It is an easy way to develop the concept of change. Guy Fawkes' failed attempt to blow up Parliament is celebrated each November. Teachers of infants have wanted to explain its importance but do not know how to. What is 'Parliament'? Why should 'Catholics' want to blow it up? Parents and teachers are bound to have to face up to explanations of the two World Wars and the conflict in Ireland, by using the past. Children of 7 to 8 will not be put off by being told to wait until they are 9 to understand it, since they are regularly confronted by these issues in the media. Certain advertisers use historical char-

acters to get over their message. Children are bombarded by advertisements from television, hoardings in streets and undergrounds, food packets and comics. Paul Noble amusingly reminds us of the advertisement on the District Line of the London underground showing the figure of Henry VIII: 'A Return to Tower Hill, please' with the graffiti added 'and a single for the wife'.[8] Henry's execution of two of his six wives has to be known for this advertisement and addition to be appreciated.

Another outward-looking need of young children is to develop an interest in people and tolerance of their point of view. The past is concerned with the interaction of people and events all over the world. If a young child can begin a life-long interest in Roman remains, Red Indians or Mogul emperors, to give only a

4

. . . and a single for the wife

Figure 1.2 *'A return to Tower Hill, please . . .' from P. Noble,* Curriculum Planning in Primary History

few examples, he will always have a leisure interest and be a frequenter of libraries. Eight to 9 year olds have a passion for specific facts which build up personal identity. John West has proved that 6 year olds have more patience and determination to work out a tricky piece of palaeography (old handwriting) than older children. Their learning of the alphabet and how to read is so recent that this is only another challenge to be pursued regardless of time pressure. This can also lead to an interest in other alphabets, which can be of value in multicultural education, learning a foreign language and even in the inventing of an alphabet.

Interest in the past is often fired by one imaginative experience or story well told by the teacher, heard on a radio or television programme, or read in a story book. The good story has a great influence on both children and adults. Television announcers and journalists as a profession talk of getting 'a good story', gossip is a good story, and novelists such as P. G. Wodehouse, Dorothy L. Sayers and Agatha Christie sell well because their narrative provides 'a good story'. There are many exciting real-life dramas from the past which start young children off on a life-long study of one particular person or event. Some examples might be Mary Queen of Scots, the marches of Garibaldi, the traumatic experiences of Anne Frank and the imprisonment of Martin Niemöller. In the same way, the bedtime story told or read to pre-school children can lead to an interest in the past. Unfortunately, most stories suitable for this pre-school age range depict imaginary characters of a 'once upon a time' nature such as Peter Rabbit and Toad of Toad Hall.

History fulfils the practical needs of children

If the past can help to foster the inward and outward-looking needs of young children it can also fulfil practical needs through the use of concepts and skills specific to history. This is especially true of the sense of sequence or time. John Slater calls this 'a sense of history'. This involves 'a concern for evidence' so that children are always asking the question 'how do I know'? and looking for different types of evidence from artefacts (old objects), oral evidence, pictures, plans and maps, and written evidence (however slight). A sense of history is also concerned with change and difference through looking at different periods of the past in comparison with the present. Young children before the age of 9 find the comparison between different historical periods unrelated to the present almost impossible to understand, as Piaget experienced. There are also similarities between different periods of the past because all periods are concerned with human beings and their feelings and motivation. We have altered relatively little through the ages. Study of the past teaches other concepts and ideas but these two are especially important and possible to instil into young children. Such understanding breaks down generation and racial barriers and helps to give children a feeling and respect for old objects.

In spite of much previous research to the contrary, the last ten years have shown that young children can begin to develop a sense of time. A study of the past, with constant use of simple and gradually more advanced sequence-lines, first gives children of 5 to 7 an idea of sequence (what comes before what) with no dates. This can be developed, even at the age of 6, into a beginners' time-line, using two, then more dates and talking about 'centuries'. By the age of 9, children should be able to cope with the concept of about 1,000 years in time. Only a study of the past, of all areas of the curriculum can do this.

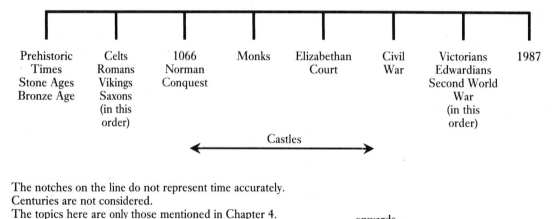

The notches on the line do not represent time accurately.
Centuries are not considered.
The topics here are only those mentioned in Chapter 4.
This could also be used by children aged 6–7 studying Victorians ⎯ onwards ⟶

Figure 1.3 *Simple sequence/time-line of topics studied by children aged 7 to 9*

Thus the past can mean many things to the young child. As I wrote some years ago:

One is that *people* existed and *events* happened before I was born, that is five, six, seven or eight years ago. Another is that these existed and happened not only around me at home and at school but in a much *wider world* (here there is a link with the concept of place). Thirdly, these people and events *change* with time (e.g. growing old) and are different from me and from each other. Fourthly, the *present* (now) and the *past* (then) are *continuous* . . . Finally, 'the past' is so huge that I find out about it in many different ways: looking, feeling, talking, drawing, reading, writing. If a child of 8 realises that these five factors make up the past, he will have a wider and deeper understanding of himself in society.[9]

This chapter started with the irony of the one area of the curriculum essentially concerned with real, individual human beings not being systematically taught in most first schools. It has then looked at the reasons for this unacceptable situation. Finally, a call has been made for the teaching and learning of history in such schools. The essential reasons are the help it gives to children in finding their own identity, the knowledge it gives them of the society in which they will become adults and the interest it can provide for a lifetime of searching, observing and reading about one area of the past. At the same time, such learning enables children to see themselves and their own particular interest in the perspective of time.

Notes

1. Slater, J. (1978) 'Why History?', *Trends*, Spring 1978, p. 4.
2. West, J. (1978) 'Young Children's Awareness of the Past', *Trends*, Spring 1978, p. 8.
3. DES (1978) *Primary Education in England*. London: HMSO.
4. DES (1967) *Children and their Primary Schools* (The Plowden Report). London: HMSO.
5. Marwick, A. (1970) *The Nature of History*, p. 13. London: Macmillan.
6. Collingwood, R. G. (1946) *The Idea of History*, p. 10. Oxford: Oxford University Press.
7. Slater, J. (1978) op. cit., p. 5.
8. Noble, P. (1985) *Curriculum Planning in Primary History*, p. 11, TH57, Historical Association.
9. Blyth, J. E. (1981) 'Helping Young Children to Understand the Past', *Early Childhood*, November 1981, p. 5.

2 Some ideas from research and development

Research and writing on young children's understanding of the past is rare, if not non-existent in the age range of 5 to 9. The inhibitions exhibited in the evaluation of the humanities generally are intensified when teaching history to 5 to 9 year old children. For example, A. V. Kelly believes that the evaluation of skill objectives is not so appropriate for humanities disciplines because success or failure, which are easy to check, are not always synonymous with understanding.[1] So far, few other means of evaluation suitable for an understanding of the past have been found and more research is badly needed in this area of the curriculum. My own work has been concerned with historical concept formation and teaching strategies.

The work of psychologists must not be overlooked in the sphere of historical concept formation. Jean Piaget's view that children aged 5 to 8 remain in the pre-operational stage of thinking may need to be accepted with some modifications but it is not encouraging. (See pp. 25–7 for more discussion of this.) J. S. Bruner's idea of a spiral curriculum is more constructive. He maintains that the same concepts can be taught in different but equally intellectually honest ways throughout the primary school. Some more recent research has borne this out. The ability of young children to be 'persistent and logical thinkers', even at 4, has been indicated by Margaret Donaldson[2] and Barbara Tizard,[3] though not specifically in relation to the past. John West's large-scale research has shown that young children (aged 6) can begin to understand such concepts as sequence and evidence if suitable strategies are used.[4] Hilary Cooper used the murder of Thomas à Becket to test concept formation in children aged 7 to 11. She came to the conclusion that 'genuine' historical thinking is possible within this age range, but that it is pre-operational in Piaget's terminology and 'must be fostered by the teaching of concrete experiences, use of narrative, visits and artefacts before it is understood'. She found that historical concepts do not develop as part of everyday vocabulary; they develop to some extent as a function of maturation and intelligence, and that a big leap forward takes place at 9+. I found that this step forward could take place somewhat earlier, during the ninth year. In Hilary Cooper's view, many concepts are developed by children having the confidence to guess when problem-solving. This obviously gives intellectual children with confidence a great advantage.[5] Hilary Cooper further interprets her findings as follows:[6]

A RESEARCH PROJECT INVESTIGATING YOUNG CHILDREN'S THINKING IN HISTORY

In my research I attempted to trace the growth of historical thinking in primary school children. I tested eighteen children (six of 7+, six of 9+ and six of 11+). Each age-group spanned a broad range of ability on standardised tests. The children listened in pairs to a tape-recorded story of the murder of Thomas à Becket (D. C. Douglas and D. W. Greenway, *English Historical Documents* II, Eyre and Methuen, 1953, pp. 698–776). Then they played two games.

The first game was called 'Murder'. Each child was given a sheet of paper divided horizontally into five sections, labelled Becket, Henry II, knights, monks and the Pope. It was divided vertically into two columns, headed, 'Case for the Prosecution' and 'Case for the Defence'. There was a section at the bottom for the 'Judge's Summing Up'. Each child was asked to write, in the first column, any reason why each of the people as groups involved might have helped to cause the murder, and to write in the opposite column anything they could say in their defence (see Figure 2.1).

The children's answers showed there was a gradual increase, depending firstly on age, and secondly on intelligence, in their ability to form logical arguments, and to see different points of view. The seven year olds saw the murder as caused solely by one of the 'suspects', usually the knights. They tried to use the words 'because', and to

SUSPECT	CASE FOR THE PROSECUTION	CASE FOR THE DEFENCE
KNIGHTS		
MONKS		
BECKET		
POPE		
KING HENRY II		
SUMMING UP		

Figure 2.1 *Example of child's Answer Sheet is given for Test 1*

give reasons to support what they said, but these were almost always simple and illogical. They might say that the knights were guilty, 'because they were nasty people', or they killed Becket, 'because he was cruel'.

The nine year olds were able to form logical arguments and to see the event in a more complex way. They could see that several of the 'suspects' were involved, and the reasons they gave took account of the personalities of Becket and the king; three-quarters of them said that Henry was proud, and Becket was stubborn. They were less dogmatic and more likely to say 'I think', or 'perhaps'. As one nine year old said, 'The knights didn't have to kill Becket'. However, in working out who was to blame, their judgement was often influenced by the violence of the crime. The knights were guilty. They did the deed. The brain turned on the floor; it would have required a strong stomach, either to do the deed or to look at it. This indicates a violent man. Only a knight would have a sword!

By eleven years old some of the children could argue the case for both prosecution and defence of the same 'suspect'. 'The knights were guilty because they should not have jumped to conclusions, but I suppose they did the right thing. Becket was a nuisance. He deserved it.' The reasons they gave to support their case sometimes looked for motives for the murder. Some made a distinction between what Henry II said and what he meant; one child wondered if his sorrow afterwards was sincere; another thought Becket might have wanted to be a saint.

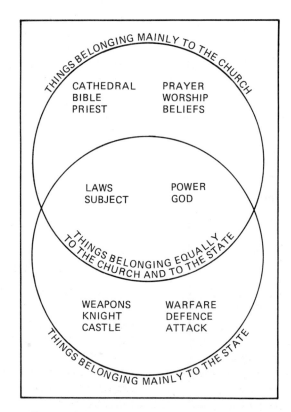

Figure 2.2 *Most logical placements for Test 2*

The second game was a card game. Overlapping circles labelled 'Church' and 'State' were drawn on a board (see Figure 2.2). Each child was given sixteen words to put into the right places on the board in order to find out what the quarrel between Becket and the king was really about. 'Knight' and 'castle' belonged in the 'state' section, and 'priest' and 'cathedral' to the 'church', but 'laws', 'power' and 'subject' should have been placed in the intersection because church and state wanted control of them.

This game showed that not even the eleven year olds really understood what the power struggle was about. Nevertheless, it did show that there is a gradual development in children's vocabulary between seven and eleven; that new ideas are learned gradually through guessing; that abstract concepts are more difficult to learn; and, most importantly, that the words which belong to history, rather than everyday vocabulary, need to be specially taught.

What, then, were the implications for my teaching when I returned to the classroom? Firstly, although these tests were artificially contrived in order to analyse children's historical thinking, they made me aware of the kinds of situations on which I could focus, in order to get the children to discuss, support their arguments, and see different points of view. This leads them to look for the reasons why things happened, and at the same time to realise that there is much that they cannot be certain about and may never know. The tests also showed me the kinds of answer I could expect at different ages. There are lots of opportunities for class discussion in which the teacher can introduce and use selected historical vocabulary. This can lead to group discussion, role-play and writing plays, letters and diaries explaining different viewpoints. This is what history is all about. The difficulty lies in finding factual evidence about real people who really lived in places which still exist and the problem which actually confronted them.

Hilary Cooper, Greenvale Primary School, Croydon.

The more specific sequence/time concept has been the subject of three recent studies. My own work is discussed in a later part of the book (Chapter 3, pp. 23–8, 30 and Chapter 5, pp. 50–4. Valerie Bone worked with a wider age range of children (5 to 13) and found that the meaning of historical terms must be consciously taught (knowing the *words* 'year', 'century' and so on was not enough), that as children advanced up the primary school their increased knowledge demanded greater practice in sequencing to avoid confusion, and the less able children could sequence quite well if artefacts and picture postcards were used.[7] Gill Aslett has worked on sequencing in the rural environment which involved the seasons of the year and the farming cycle of activities. She used pictures of landscape in the four seasons and visits to farms with 7 to 9 year olds as well as older primary children.[8] Gill Aslett explains her work in her own words:

UNDERSTANDING SEQUENCE IN THE RURAL ENVIRONMENT

The connection between time and sequence is an interacting one both in history and science. Understanding that the Romans were here before the Normans means that children also know that they were further away in time from the present day. In history, *chronology* links time and sequence with a linear 'time-line'. But in the physical world, sequences are often cyclic; with plant-growth and the seasons there is an *order* of things which will repeat itself when one cycle is completed.

Just as young children can approach the concept of time in history through their family 'time-line', so they often first equate the seasons with their personal calendar. Winter means Christmas, and also cold and snow; summer means holidays, and usually warmth, blue skies and bright flowers. They know quite well which season their birthday is in, and that each time this comes, they are one year older. But how and when do they become fully aware of the seasonal *sequence*? It seems probable that this becomes clearer as their perception of the rural environment develops. Research into environmental perception, largely based in the urban environment, indicates that it is developed by direct contact and active involvement in the world (R. C. Moore, 1986). I am finding that children's contact with farmland, which makes up over 70% of England and Wales, is limited, and am therefore very pleased that the farming community is becoming more welcoming to schools.

My research involves the use which primary and middle schools make of a farm link. Initially I worked with a small rural primary school, where a class of 6–7 year olds made a number of visits to two farms in the village which had agreed to be linked to the school. The childrens' observations on the visits, and their talk with the farmers, gave rise to a range of classroom work across the curriculum, including science-based experiments with seed and soil, which had all the purpose and reality derived from first-hand experience (Aslett and Roberts, 1986). Particularly, we found that the children developed an understanding of the sequence of growth, and were able to connect their results from planting seeds in the classroom and school grounds with the larger scale of events in the surrounding farms.

The following year I joined a class of 7–9 year olds in a small town, and I wanted some way of reviewing *how* the children's grasp of the sequence of events in the countryside developed during their work on farming, and how the visits to a farm influenced this. I decided to use two picture sequences, which the children could put in order, as a way of reviewing their perception of the farmed environment, and knowledge of the seasonal sequence. This activity was undertaken twice – once before we embarked on any farm visits, and again at the end of the summer term. One set of pictures was of a farmer ploughing, drilling and harvesting. Two-thirds of the class identified the ploughing and harvesting pictures, and half guessed that the drill was 'sowing the seeds', but the taped comments indicated that only a fifth of the children really understood the sequence of these activities. The other set was of farmland in spring, summer, autumn and winter. Only a third of the children put the pictures in the right order, which would appear to indicate that the seasonal sequence is by no means clear to this age group. However, when I listened to their taped comments, it seemed that another third of the class knew the sequence, but that their perception of the pictures varied. The spring picture was of a ewe and lambs with the bare hedgerow behind; several children put this as autumn. The autumn picture was a stubble field edged with beeches turning brown and red, while summer had fully grown wheat; the shorter stubble confused the issue, and 'It's spring; the leaves are on, and the corn's growing', explained one child. Finally, one-third of the children could neither recall the seasonal sequence nor order the pictures.

The value of this exercise to me, and

to the teacher, was mainly diagnostic — it gave us a clear idea of how the children perceived farmland, and helped with planning the work to follow farm visits. I think such picture sequences may also have an instructional benefit in themselves, in that they focus the child's attention on sequencing, and encourage them to find reasons for their choice of order. The results need careful interpretation, and there are many problems involved in finding a representative set of pictures, but I am continuing the activity with another school, and again, find the results very revealing.

Gill Aslett, Research Student at Cambridge Institute of Education

References
ASLETT, G. and ROBERTS, M. (1986) 'Using farm links – a small rural primary takes to the fields', *Primary Teaching Studies*, Vol. 1, No. 3, June 1986.
MOORE, R. C. (1986) *Childhood's Domain. Play and Place in Child Development.* Beckenham: Croom Helm.

Sequencing of this sort helps historical sequencing and narrative story-telling, although it differs in that the seasonal and farming year cycles are sure to repeat themselves whereas historical sequencing is seldom repeated. This causes uncertainty for young children but the essence of all historical material is its uniqueness. Therefore, children have to be encouraged to make the calculated guess or 'hunch', to use Bruner's happy word. The work of John West, Hilary Cooper, Valerie Bone and Gill Aslett, as well as my own, is encouraging, in that it suggests possible and practical guidelines and so should stimulate primary teachers to be cautiously optimistic as to the ability of their children to form historical concepts.

The whole area of imagination, empathy and feeling for others is less easy to tackle as it is so much a matter of opinion on the part of the research worker. Recent research has been undertaken by Sophie Blakeway[9] with 8 to 9 year old children using the writing and production of a play on the Peasants' Revolt of 1381, and making models of a medieval village in the fourteenth century. These activities showed the imaginative insight of children and 'the seriousness of purpose' evident during their work. Peter Knight is currently undertaking a large piece of research on *Children's Understanding of People in the Past*[10] which involves imagination and how much sense children make of people in the past (preferred to the less precise term 'empathy'). His study is involved with 6, 9 and 10 year olds with some reference to junior/secondary children.

UNDERSTANDING PEOPLE IN THE PAST

History is about people. Sometimes that fact gets lost when we plan for source-based work to develop children's skills. We can forget that we wrestle with the sources *in order to* try and understand people in the past.

But should we expect 5–9s to try and understand people in the past? After all they are only in the concrete operational stage; they have limited experience of the world of grown-ups (Furth, 1980); and knowledge about past peoples is usually to be obtained by reading, a skill which they are just learning to master. So, might it not be better to stick to 'pre-disciplinary' activities, or confine work on the past to the study of its obvious, physical remains?

Many teachers of the 5–9s will find it easy to reconcile that sort of work with their educational beliefs. However, I want to suggest that these children can go beyond pre-disciplinary activities and the physically concrete: they can make some sense of the doings of people in the past. Nevertheless, we may decide that the 5–9s should only do

13

recent, local history; but if that is the decision, it needs to be justified and that cannot be done by saying that other work on the past is too hard for children of that age.

I shall try to make my case in two ways. To begin with I want to return to the claims that the 5–9s are not able to reason about people in history. It is true that they will generally be at the stage of concrete operations. A little thought about their worlds of fantasy and imagination will remind us that even concrete thinkers do not think only about the *physically* concrete. Their experience of the adult world is limited but no more so than in 101 other realms which are cheerfully tackled in school. It is not simple to ensure that young children gain the information they need, but pictures and stories are powerful approaches and some publishers are trying other means. In short, children may be able to do more than is sometimes assumed.

My other line of argument draws upon a classroom study. I took one class of 33 7–9 year olds and another of 23 5–7 year olds, each for a term. Before I started teaching, I talked with each child about five history problems. Their answers were used to split each class into two, matched groups. The term's work was on the Middle Ages. The topic was chosen mainly because the differences between medieval and modern cultures are substantial enough to provide a fair test of children's ability to understand people in the past. The topic was guided by a best-selling school book on the period which is full of vivid pictures. In each class one of the groups (called the 'Text' group), took a basically factual approach. The emphasis was upon describing what people did and how they lived. While it was impossible entirely to avoid explaining their actions, attention was concentrated on describing, for example, the Peasants'

Revolt, monastic life, castle building and medicine. The other group (the 'Explanation' group), took the same time to cover the same materials. However, I badgered them with the question 'Why?' They still had to grasp the 'facts' but they were also prompted to try to explain them: why revolt? be a monk? build (and then replace) earth and wood castles? trepan? Some time was spent, too, in trying to take on the perspective of others, by describing a Crusader from a Turkish point of view, for example. Similar teaching methods were used with both groups. In the belief that with the 5–9s writing can get in the way of thinking, I used oral work – stories, drama, group work, and role play – as much as possible. We produced little that could go on the wall.

I was trying to find out three things. First, I wanted to know whether a course could be put together that would encourage children to reason about people in the past. Secondly, I wanted to see if the 5–9s could cope with it. Thirdly, I wanted to see whether the course would improve their ability to think about people in history.

To the first two questions the answer is that it proved possible to take a fact-flogging account of the Middle Ages and to use it to get children talking about the actions of past peoples. There were no tears of frustration, such as we sometimes see with, say, number work, but there were signs of enjoyment. Most of the children showed understanding, albeit childish understanding.

Figure 2.3 answers the third question. Within a week of the course finishing the children were interviewed on a set of 11 problems which required them to work out explanations of actions in the Middle Ages and other periods. Their answers were each given a mark so that powerful statistical procedures could be used to analyse them. *By themselves these numbers are meaningless.* Figure

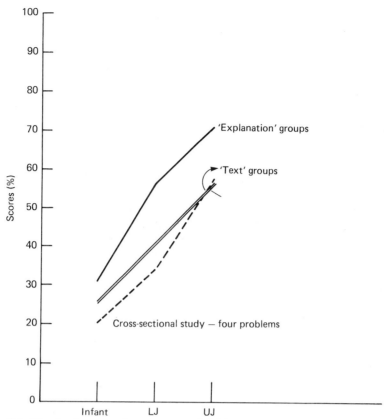

Figure 2.3 *The development of some aspects of children's understanding of people in the past*

6 must be read cautiously. The lower two lines show a pattern of development established in an earlier study of 71 children in four primary schools. The 'Text' groups display a similar pattern, which implies that their work on the Middle Ages did not improve their understanding of the actions of people in the past. The explanation course appears to have little impact upon the Infants but the Lower Juniors did benefit to a degree which has less than a 5% probability of happening by chance. The data on the Upper Juniors are added to reinforce the point.

I conclude by noting one claim and by making one of my own. It has been said that trying to understand people in the past is similar to trying to understand people in the present (Collingwood, 1946, p. 219). On such a basis, Thompson (1983) has argued that 'empathy' (which I take to include trying to understand people in history) is an important part of the curriculum in the early years of schooling and one which may be furthered through work on the past. Thompson's is a claim about the value of developing the 'skill' of 'empathy': mine is that the 5–9s can cope with work which asks them to reason about the motives of characters in history and that the levels of understanding which the 7–9s (and older children) show may be improved by appropriate teaching.

Teachers, then, are faced with a choice. They could make thought about people's reasoning a part of topic and history work. Alternatively, they could decide not to – perhaps because my brief report is unconvincing, or because it may seem to imply a style of teaching which they reject. What is not permissible, I hope, is the argument that this

15

sort of work cannot be done with the 5–9s and that, even if it could, the children could neither cope with it nor benefit from it.

It can, they can and some did.

Peter Knight, S. Martin's College, Lancaster.

References

COLLINGWOOD, R. G. (1946) *The Idea of History.* Oxford: Oxford University Press.

FURTH, H. G. (1980) *The World of Grown Ups.* New York: Elsevier.

THOMPSON, F. (1983) 'Empathy: an aim and a skill to be developed!', *Teaching History* 37, pp. 22–6.

water

food

food

heat

water

shelter

shelter

heat

What did Early Man need to survive?
What do we need to survive?

Figure 2.4 *Drawings of Early Man by 5 to 7 year olds*

Essex LEA sponsored a Curriculum Extension Project[11] for pupils of 5 to 7 years on *Working with Early Man* (see Figure 2.4). An infant headteacher, Barbara Bexley, planned this project for the very able children in her class, and seems to have 'extended' them to a considerable extent. The project integrated mathematics, language, science, art, drama and music but no mention was made of the key disciplines relating to 'Early Man' of history, archaeology or zoology! The children worked on the project from worksheets, either alongside their peers or in a specialised group of their own. The pamphlet explains the project,

16

gives a very full list of resources and detailed information for the teacher to be adapted for worksheets for the children. Some of the topics undertaken are 'Making a Cave Painting', 'Houses and Homes', 'From Summer to Winter', 'Body Language' (as Early Man had no other language), 'Steps in Time', and 'Shoebox History'. 'Steps in Time' asked the children to make a staircase of the different types of Early Man which they had found out from books as a group. The staircase would look like Figure 2.5. 'Shoebox History' involved putting all the small things the children themselves use today in a shoebox and labelling them. This box was to be discovered in the distant future. They then made a similarly labelled shoe box for Early Man from replicas

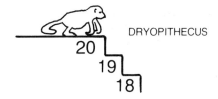

Figure 2.5 *Steps in Time*

and models. 'From Summer to Winter' and 'From Hot to Cold' involved making a chart of prehistoric animals before and after their coats for the winter had been grown. Figure 2.6 is the diagram used to start them off. This project helped children to reach a very high standard in thinking and in practical work and to read and consult books on a considerable scale.

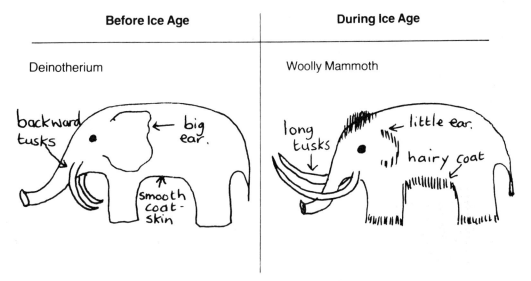

Figure 2.6 *From Summer to Winter*

Less work has been done or thought given to research into teaching techniques, though all the researchers and innovators mentioned have been involved in seeking and trying out new ways of teaching. In devising tests for concept evaluation in my own study, I was able to experiment with some interesting teaching techniques. All four concept tests used different methods of teaching. Genuine Edwardian school artefacts were used for 'evidence', two large coloured pictures of a street at different periods for 'change', fourteen coloured postcards for 'sequence' and a taped story of the Massacre of Peterloo for 'power' (see Chapter 3, p. 26). More details of how these strategies were used are given elsewhere in this book.

The idea of using artefacts for introducing children to work on historical evidence is by no means new; many primary schools have used either genuine or replicated artefacts. John Davis writes of his work on these lines in Chapter 5 of this book.[12] Martin Forrest researched with two teachers and children aged 5 to 6 and 8 to 9 in the use of artefacts.[13] The 5 to 6 year olds could sort out objects in terms of chronology as they placed objects in the correct time sequence. They could also develop an argument in support of an idea after handling the artefacts: an Edwardian flat iron led to the idea of heating the iron on the open fire and thus to a discussion about the hard work involved, the slowness of this method and the need for an open grate and coal. The 8 to 9 year olds used three cases of objects covering a wide span of years and borrowed from the City Museum, Bristol.[14]

Figure 2.7 *Butter 'hands' from Avon Resources for Learning Development Unit*

Videotapes of the lessons showed that the children improved after the second and third cases had been used, that more history was learnt after the research than before, that oral work was improved particularly by using difficult objects (this bears out Carol Dweck's work, see Chapter 3, p. 28) and that the children used reference books related to the objects more effectively after the third box of artefacts.

Susan Perrin experimented with four artefacts in her class of 24 6 year olds, divided into six groups of four.[15] Her topic was 'Hot and Cold' and the four artefacts were concerned with 'keeping ourselves warm'. They were a Victorian copper warming pan of 1860, an Edwardian stone hot water bottle of 1905, a rubber hot water bottle of 1968 and an electric blanket of 1985. She chose these objects as people used them over a long period of time and so enabled her to test sequencing of events at the same time. She introduced the first two artefacts wrapped up to add to the excitement (as Martin Forrest's teacher did) and then all of them as a group. The reaction of the six groups naturally varied but they were responsive and full of ideas of the whole. The warming pan and the stone hot water bottle were the most difficult to identify. The stone hot water bottle was identified first so as not to give any clue to chronology. Most children used possibility and probability terms to reach positive conclusions; for example, the warming pan was said to hold hot water to warm a bed until the holes in the lid showed that this was impossible, therefore hot coal became the correct solution. In many cases the children understood the concepts but lacked the correct language to explain their meaning; thus the 'pattern' on the stone hot water bottle and its 'stopper' caused difficulties. This language problem was largely overcome by discussion in small groups of four but 'more specialised historical and mathematical vocabulary should

Figure 2.8 *Six year olds examining a copper warming pan*

be taught'.[16] The children were 'able to follow a logical argument to a reasoned conclusion'.[17] They used guesswork to place the four objects in correct sequence, finding the order of the two hot water bottles the most difficult. They could not master the number of years between the objects; the relationship between number and dates begins to emerge only at about 8 years of age. As is usual with young children, the researcher tape-recorded their discussions and went over them afterwards. She found the use of artefacts an excellent way to introduce historical evidence and sequencing to infants.

Another piece of research from the same stable[18] links the specialised work on concepts, sequencing and artefacts to the broader issues of historical resources for the integrated curriculum. Stephen Tofts observed work in five infant schools in the Bristol area to find out what materials were being used and to what effect. He had been directed by Peter Gilliat, then Humanities Adviser for Avon, to schools in which teachers were enthusiastic about the past. The approaches he found were conventional and suitable; family history, artefacts, a study of the local area and Victorian schools compared with our own. The methods used were mostly conventional but sound ones; the use of old photographs, visits and drawing. But two methods seem to have produced very advanced work for 6 year olds; they are the reading of an 1881 census return and imaginative and competent writing by the children. Handling of an old silver watch led one child to write:

> If I was a woman a hundred years ago, sometimes I would wear this silver watch around my neck and I would wear something like a blouse and a long skirt to go with it.[19]

Stephen Tofts thought that more use should have been made of stories, sequence lines and

19

library skills. He regretted that few schools have thought out guidelines for teaching history in the infant school. He came to the conclusion that history was not too difficult for 5 to 7 year olds and that it should be part of an integrated course.

The teaching strategy of story-telling has been much neglected, especially in the area of learning about the past. Although not specifically concerned with historical sources, Barry Wade has experimented with story-telling in 10 West Midlands schools for two terms, followed up after two years.[20] The schools included five nursery schools and five infant/junior schools; the parents of the children were also involved. The experimental groups made progress in telling stories and even more progress in recounting a story of their own choice. When the children were retold stories the researchers had first told them, it was found that children's powers of narrative, understanding of the past and general confidence had developed. The one-to-one relationship of parent to child led to rapid progress. I too found this to be true in my tape-recorded story of the 'Massacre of Peterloo', used for the testing of the concept of 'power'. At first, the children, even in a one-to-one relationship, could not follow the story, but after asking them to retell me the story and listen to the tape again, the answers to my questions were successful on the whole.

The dearth of research into young children's understanding of the past may lead to the conclusion that methods of research have not been as suitable as they might have been. During the last decade, new methods of evaluation have been used with helpful results for the humanities area of the curriculum. In a chapter on 'Techniques of Evaluation', Stephen Steadman suggests that pupil's oral opinion and reaction should be considered as a source of evaluation as well as observation. 'The younger the child the less his opinions are likely to be sought – understandably so as teacher assessment of the reactions of children under eleven is heavily relied upon unless the methods of direct observation . . . are used.'[21] This is important for research with young children who cannot complete a questionnaire reliably and are usually tested in a one-to-one situation. I used this method of oral opinion and observation when asking children which of my four tests they preferred as teaching methods.

Teachers connected with the Bulmershe College of Higher Education, under the leadership of Mike Wilson, have been using the method of 'triangulation' in which researcher, teacher and pupils are all involved in the work, and their joint views contribute to the final results. His work with primary school children owes a debt to the broader research of Clem Adelman[22] and his colleagues. In *Inside the Classroom Vol. II*,[23] case studies are described in which the researcher observes and tape-records an hour's lesson and then obtains the reaction of the teacher who taught it and the children who were the subjects. The lessons used as case studies were not connected with history and some were carried out with older juniors, but triangulation laid bare teaching strategies which were ineffective and occasions when children were confused. Mike Wilson wondered whether 7 to 8 year old children were too young to respond readily to his questions and to give satisfactory replies. This may be accounted for by the fact that he questioned children in groups of six instead of one-to-one and also that he was questioning them about their teacher rather than their views on the material taught.

Observation in the primary classroom as a research technique has also been used by Michael Armstrong[24] and above all by the ORACLE team from the University of Leicester.[25] Put briefly, the researchers found their class teaching involved more problem solving and pupil–teacher interaction than individual learning which was most often the collection of factual material by the child. They advocated probing class teaching for a third of every lesson and more structured group work for the remaining two-thirds. The ORACLE project favoured research into teaching strategies by observation. 'Only observational studies can supply information about a teacher's style. At their best questionnaires tell us about a teacher's aims and offer global descriptions in terms of strategies.'[26] Using the same techniques of observation, Neville Bennett and his team were concerned with the quality of learning for 6 to 7 year olds with 16 teachers.[27] The researchers found that teachers were not successful at 'matching' tasks to pupils' ability and age range. The matching deteriorated as the term advanced, high attainers were underestimated and low attainers overestimated. This bears out the view that from the age of 7 to that of 11 teachers seem to teach the same material in the same way, and are not concerned with individual pupils' differential progress in the humanities area of the curriculum. In the words of Bennett, 'This staple diet of little new knowledge and large amounts of practice was rarely varied to include tasks which required either discovery or construction of new or different ways of perceiving problems, or the application of existing knowledge and skills to new contexts.'[28] Bennett and his team believe that class management receives scant attention in literature.

Those holding the reins of power in primary schools should be more concerned about this area of the curriculum generally. There are recent signs that there is a move in the direction of specialist help to primary teachers. Both the 1978 Primary Survey and the 1982 *Education 5 to 9* Report stress the need for more expertise in the classroom in relation to the humanities. In an excellent article, Carolyn Steadman[29] eloquently summarises the present dilemma for primary schools in relation to the past:

First of all, there is an uneasiness within progressive child-centred education about the relevance of the past to young children, a reluctance to teach history, which presents no concrete material for children to manipulate, and its consequent absorption into other curriculum areas. Secondly, there is a reluctance on the part of academics (all academics, not just historians) to engage with the questions that are raised by considering children in the early

stages of acquiring the cognitive framework for a discipline.

This account of recent research and writing helpful to those of us who are interested in young children understanding the past, indicates the need for more work to be done if progress is to be made. An encouraging development is that new methods of research such as observation and co-operation with teachers, and even pupils, are more suitable for research than the older statistical methods. In his review of Stephen Rowland's *The Enquiring Classroom*,[30] A. V. Kelly applauds the book as pointing the way to:

a new and more productive model of educational research, one which eschews those spurious attempts to make 'Scientific' measurements of educational activities and which see research in terms of the 'shared insights' of the only people who can fully understand the complexities of an educational encounter, those who are themselves engaged in it.[31]

Notes

1. Kelly, A. V. (1982) *The Curriculum – Theory and Practice.* London: Harper and Row.
2. Donaldson, M. (1978) *Children's Minds.* London: Fontana.
3. Tizard, B. and Hughes, M. (1984) *Young Children Learning.* London: Fontana.
4. West, J. (1981) *Children's Awareness of the Past.* Unpublished PhD, Keele University.
5. Cooper, H. (1982) *Questions Arising in an Attempt to Interpret the Historical Thinking of Primary School Children According to Theories of Cognitive Development.* Diploma in Child Development, University of London.
6. More details about this research may be found in Cooper, H. (1983) 'From Marbles to Murder', *Teaching History*, June 1983, No. 36, Historical Association.
7. Bone, V. A. (1984) *An Investigation into Children's Understanding of Historical Frequence.* Diploma, Froebel College, Roehampton.
8. Aslett, G. (1987) *Using farm links with primary and middle schools: an enquiry into children's learning and the factors contributing to it resulting from repeated visits to a linked farm.* MEd Dissertation, Cambridge Institute of Education.
9. Blakeway, S. (1986) 'The development of empathy and historical understanding through imaginative work',

History and the Primary School, Greater Manchester Primary Contact, Special Issue No. 6, pp. 25–30.

10. Knight, P. (1988) *Children's Understanding of People in the Past*. Forthcoming PhD thesis, University of Lancaster.

11. Essex Department of Education, Essex Curriculum Extension Project Infant Series (5–7 years) No. 2, *Working with Early Man*. Available from Education Department, PO Box 47, Threadneedle House, Market Road, Chelmsford, Essex CM1 1LD.

12. See pp. 65–8; also Davis, J. (1986) 'Artefacts in the Primary School (with 10 to 11 year olds)', *Teaching History*, No. 45, June 1986, Historical Association.

13. Forrest, M. St. John (1983) *The Teacher as Researcher – the use of historical artefacts in the primary school*. MEd Dissertation, University of Bath.

14. The City Museum, Bristol, has taken great initiative in preparing and lending cases of genuine artefacts representative of different periods to schools. This work has linked teachers, Avon Education Authority and the University of Bristol School of Education.

15. Perrin, S. (1986) *Using Historical Objects to Stimulate Talk with Infants*. Dissertation for Diploma in Advanced Studies in Education, University of Bristol.

16. Ibid., p. 52.

17. Ibid., p. 1.

18. Tofts, S. G. C. (1984) *History in the Infants School: an empirical study of the way in which historical material is used with infants in the integrated curriculum*. Dissertation for the Diploma in Advanced Studies in Education, University of Bristol.

19. Ibid., p. 50.

20. Wade, B. (1984) 'Story at Home and School', *Educational Review Occasional Paper 10*. University of Birmingham.

21. Steadman, S. (1976) 'Techniques of evaluation', in Tawney, D. (ed.) *Curriculum Evaluation Today: Trends and Implications*, p. 63. Schools Council Research Studies.

22. Adelman, C. (1981) *Uttering Muttering*. Oxford: Grant McIntyre.

23. Wilson, M. (1983) *Inside the Classroom Vol. II*. Bulmershe College of Higher Education.

24. Armstrong, M. (1980) *Closely Observed Children – the diary of a primary classroom* (8 to 9 year olds). Richmond: Chameleon.

25. Galton, M., Simon, B. and Croll, P. (1980) *Inside the Primary Classroom*. London: Routledge and Kegan Paul; Galton, M. and Simon, B. (eds) (1980) *Progress and Performance in the Primary Classroom*. London: Routledge and Kegan Paul.

26. Galton, M. *et al.* (1980) op. cit., p. 115.

27. Bennett, N., Desforges, C., Cockburn, A. and Wilkinson, B. (1984) *The Quality of Pupil Learning Experiences*. New Jersey: Lawrence Erlbaum Associates.

28. Ibid., p. 213.

29. Steadman, C. (1984) 'Battlegrounds: History in Primary Schools', *History Workshop*, Issue 17, Spring 1984.

30. Rowland, S. (1984) *The Enquiring Classroom*. London: Falmer Press.

31. *Times Educational Supplement*, 10 August 1984.

3 How young children learn about the past

There are many ways in which children of first-school age respond to the past and one of the most potent is looking at historical pictures. In order to investigate further this technique, I carried out a short series of investigations in some schools in and around South-West London in the years 1983–4 (see pp. 24–6).

Looking first at the concept of difference and change I used two scenes of a street in my tests on 36 5 to 9 year old children. These pictures (Figures 3.1 and 3.2) were taken from a Midland Bank calendar depicting the development of banking. One shows a street in the Middle Ages and the other a street in the early nineteenth century. It is unlikely that they show the same street but this is immaterial. I asked the children to tell me what stories they saw in the pictures, drawing on their imaginations. I asked them, 'What is happening in this picture?' In addition I asked them to say which picture happened first in the past in

Figure 3.1 *A street in the Middle Ages by Justin Todd*

Figure 3.2 *A street in the nineteenth century by Justin Todd*

time order. Finally, they answered a series of questions on the differences in the two street scenes in methods of travel, buildings and the clothes people were wearing. The children only had the two pictures as points of reference, they had not been taught about the historical periods and neither of the pictures had any connection with a modern street.

Picture reading and the concept of change

Figure 3.1 shows medieval nobles bringing money in bags to the pawnbroker in exchange for the return of their goods. In the two open-fronted shops moneylenders can be seen weighing out gold, putting money bags in a chest and keeping accounts using quill pens. The arrival of the wealthy nobles with their servants on horseback has caused a stir in the small street; animals are running in all directions, a child is crying and a woman is looking out of an upstairs window to see what the noise is about. The buildings are jettied (top floors overhanging the streets) and timberframed,

and the surface of the street is made of large stones placed in mud in a random fashion. In contrast, Figure 3.2 shows an early nineteenth-century coach drawn by one horse, money in a big box being brought to a bank (a large stone building) and passers-by being entertained by dancing dogs and a fiddler. A second building in the picture is built of brick, with a slate roof and chimneys. The street is cobbled.

The picture-reading – asking children to tell a story about each picture – proved difficult for all but the 9 year olds. This was probably because most of the children had been told, or had had read to them, stories by the teacher, but had not told stories themselves or retold the ones told by the teacher. This freedom confused the younger children. They all linked both pictures with gold and money but there was confusion beyond that. The 9 year olds had greater success, probably because of the ways they had been taught. In one school, children were encouraged to 'have a guess' and not to bother too much whether it was right. In the other school in this test, children took the initiative to *find* a story and only *used* details to help them, not as ends in themselves. These two groups were convinced that the pictures were about money, account-keeping, stealing and shops. One boy ventured that the first picture was a 'middle-aged scene'!

The sequencing of the two pictures was an easier task even though reasons for the choice sometimes altered a child's mind, which showed reasoning powers. The 8 year olds did not do as well as the 7 and 9 year olds. The 9 year olds were particularly capable and gave intelligent reasons for correct sequencing – that is that the first picture was before the second picture in time. One boy thought that the second picture was later because a violin of the shape shown in that illustration had not been invented 'in early days', when viols and virginals were used.

These two initial tasks got the children looking closely at the two pictures which prepared them for the change/difference questions. All the children found differences in forms of travel easy to understand, the first being on horseback and the second by coach, drawn by one horse. This answer needed quick observation and did not require any previous knowledge or imagination. The difference in the buildings was not so self-evident and none of the children could relate building materials to architectural styles. Differences in costume evoked more interest and knowledge, though the younger age-groups lacked the correct terminology for costume of the past. Thus many of them spoke of clothes in the first picture as being 'rags', 'torn' and 'ripped' when they meant loose-fitting, flowing medieval garments. 'Robin Hood hats' and 'magic shoes' were delightful tokens of the spirit of the age in the first picture – 'square' hats in the second picture (for top hats). A sprinkling of children believed that bright colours in clothes meant that the period was earlier and some the other way round. The knowledge that medieval clothes were drab on account of fewer dyes had not come the children's way.

The conclusion one comes to is that all age-groups could cope with change/ difference where it was obvious from the pictures, though lack of historical vocabulary limited their expression of this correct thought. The 9 year olds were better at sequencing the two pictures, the uncertainties of imagining stories from pictures and concocting coherent narrative to express their ideas.

How children learn from picture reading

These children were learning about the concept of change at the same time as being tested individually as part of my research. In fact they believed that I was 'teaching' them! The majority of them had no previous knowledge of the Middle Ages or the nineteenth century and learnt as the test proceeded. Therefore, most of them were using their senses, in this case, of eyes, ears and tongue. In addition, their feelings were involved, as all 36 children were highly motivated in a 'one-to-one' relationship with a stranger. This applied regardless of intelligence as bright, average and less able were tested in all my six schools. In a few cases, children of all age-groups used a level of logical thinking (reasoning) associated by Piaget with the 'formal operations' of older children.

In this case, the children were using their eyes to observe the two pictures. They do this regularly when watching television and the cinema screen, but few of them know how to 'picture read' carefully in order to learn, other than for entertainment purposes. Gill Aslett has found this in her research with the sequence of the seasons of the year with 7 to 9 year olds.[1] Many children noticed details in the pictures, such as the scales and pawnbroker's sign in the first picture, and the royal crest on the side of the coach in the second picture. But it was only the older, more intelligent children who realised how these details altered the story and still saw the picture as a whole. The children needed help from me as to the points of common comparison in the two pictures, such as travel, buildings and clothes. The children would have needed less help in comparing, if one of the pictures had been of a contemporary street. Learning by looking and by trained, detailed observation leads children to ask questions of themselves, their peers and their teacher. This is a particularly appropriate way of learning about the past for 6 to 7 year olds who are only beginner readers. It can also encourage 8 to 9 year olds to seek information from books and relate pictures and the written word.

The children also learnt in their change concept exercise by listening to me talking and discussing the two pictures from the points of view of sequence, story and change. This method of learning also applies to listening to the spoken word on television, radio and on tape. When testing their concept of 'power' I recorded a four minute story about the 'Massacre of Peterloo' on St Peter's Fields, Manchester, in 1819 and then asked questions about the wielding of power.[2]

Going beyond this particular piece of research there are many other ways in which children learn from oral work. Children of this age also tape-record old people's memories when studying social life in the early part of this century and then listen to the 'play-back' to gather information orally. The use of oral history in primary schools has been developed over the last ten years in a systematic and scholarly way but this effective method of studying the past can be overdone. Storytelling is well known in theory but little used in practice to teach history. 'Listening at the feet'

Figure 3.3 *The Massacre of Peterloo (City of Manchester Central Library)*

of the teacher at the end of the infant day can introduce children to many parts of the past and lead to discussion, role play and practical activity.[3] Remembering also helps children to learn sequencing of events. Which 'bit' have you forgotten for the story to make sense? This technique applies particularly to the tape of Peterloo which I played once before each child told the story and then a second time to add the omissions, and before answering questions. Story-telling also involves children in learning by imitation of the teachers – often called 'observational learning' or 'modelling' when the acquisition of knowledge is involved.[4]

Listening to the teacher is only one part of the whole area of teaching strategies; it also includes teaching styles and using materials and techniques appropriate to the child's stage of cognitive development. 'Where learning fails to take place, the fault lies not in the nature of the subject to be taught nor in the child himself, but in the form in which the learning experience is presented.' David Fontana's words emphasise the influence of the role of the teacher on the way children learn.[5] In other words, the child cannot learn by himself, solely by 'discovery methods'. Many teachers of 6 to 7 year olds fail to 'match' tasks to each child's development, particularly as the year advances and differences between children's capabilities become more marked.[6] Wynne Harlen also found this discrepancy in the teaching of science to primary-age children[7] Although Piaget's stages of cognitive development need not be adhered to strictly when dealing with the past, all children of 5 to 9 must work through the stages even if at different speeds, moving from pre-operational schemes to concrete operational ones. Therefore, at about 7 children need to handle genuine artefacts and/or concrete replicas of the past and discuss them with their teachers. To provide appropriate resources and teaching strategies, teachers must 'pick up signals from the children' which cannot usually be anticipated.[8]

Listening to the teacher on the part of the child is closely linked with discussion between teacher and child, which was a major way of learning in the picture work discussed earlier. This is part of language development, though teachers should extend everyday ordinary vocabulary to include specific historical words such as 'fossil', 'bygone' and 'monarch'.[9] Two contemporary researchers, J. S. Bruner and Joan Tough, have encouraged teachers of young children to 'talk' to their children more, particularly in a 'one-to-one' relationship, to ask leading questions and use the children's answers to promote thinking a step further. Bruner thinks that at about the age of 6 or 7 a child's language begins to be used in problem-solving and is not entirely dependent upon carrying out concrete operations. Joan Tough believes that 'there is no doubt that the development of language is dependent on the child's interaction with others.[10] Following the psychologist Vygotsky and his successors she claims that naming (putting words to objects and thoughts) 'helped children to search for similarities and differences' and that 'words are central to the process of forming complex concepts'.[11] Such concepts include change, sequence (time), evidence and power, all so very relevant to teaching about the past. Kathy Sylva and Ingrid Lunt write of the need for a baby to hear its mother talking to it and reacting to supposed or actual responses. They write 'adult assistance may be important in learning how to take conversational turns'.[12] They say that in the pre-school years, children notice number and past/present time but cannot express them.[13] How much more true this is for 5 to 7 year olds making conversation about the past.

Two less expected aspects to emerge from my work with the 5 to 9 year olds were the high motivation and enthusiasm of most of the children and the considerable general historical knowledge which several of them possessed and which may have come from their homes. This motivation may have been stimulated by each child being chosen by the class teacher to work with me on 'special work'. It also came from the willingness to make mistakes and take it in their stride exhibited during these early years. Carol Dweck, of

Harvard University, writes that at infant school children are optimistic. 'They seem to think they will get more clever as they get older, if they learn more and work hard.' In my case, a one-to-one relationship encouraged children to 'have a go' in a way suitable to each child. Carol Dweck believes that from about 8, children need to learn to overcome problems by undertaking difficult tasks: 'I think what children learn best from, are slightly difficult tasks which they have to struggle through. They do need challenges and obstacles to bring them greater confidence.[14] The children I studied also had each task explained thoroughly, and therefore knew what was required of them. The novelty of my approach was just enough to maintain their interest and not too much to become daunting. The 9 year olds' general knowledge of the Middle Ages, transport, houses and costume enabled many of them to use their visits to museums and houses, and their own reading to maximum effect. General maturation obviously helped here. This had a snowball effect as discussion of the pictures proceeded, those children with knowledge gaining more confidence and so making progress.

Additional ways of learning

The children I studied used their senses, emotions and knowledge to understand the concept of change. Young children also learn in other ways. The three most important are activity (doing and using their hands), reading and writing and, gradually, thinking. The 1931 Hadow Report on the junior years (p. 93) urged, in its familiar comment, that the curriculum was to 'be thought of in terms of activity and experience, rather than of knowledge to be acquired and facts to be stored', and most psychologists would endorse this approach. One of the dangers of teaching about the past is that the information does not readily promote activity for young children. At present, teachers have to provide their own resources to cater for this activity. (More will be said about resources in Chapter 6.)

Two other tests I gave my 36 children involved the concepts of evidence and sequence. I used four artefacts from Victorian/Edwardian schools borrowed from the British Schools Museum at Hitchin (unfortunately now closed) – a slate and slate pencil, an abacus frame, a pair of dumb-bells, a round ruler, and an 1889 book of Bible stories of my own. In most cases the children responded well to handling the artefacts and used them thoughtfully as evidence of schooling very different from their own. In this test 7 year olds were as adept as 9 year olds, particularly if they had done previous work on artefacts. In my sequence test the children handled coloured postcards of historical personalities, buildings and transport at different periods of the past. The handling helped them to think of the correct sequence in time and put them on the table in their own sequence.[15]

Learning by doing is frequently carried out by children drawing 'historical' pictures, making their own books,[16] counting days, weeks, months and years to make 'a long time ago', and by larger enterprises such as field work,[17] looking at castles and stately homes and going on museum visits. Imaginative play, role play and drama are further very effective 'doing' activities, as are model-making and craft work. All these ways of learning become teaching strategies and will be discussed more fully in Chapter 5. These activities have always been favoured by teachers using 'discovery methods' of learning, though there has been a movement in favour of a more structured approach recently. Piaget has led the way concerning the need to handle, touch and make pictures and models and has shown that 'children . . . are not like vessels waiting to be filled up with knowledge[18] but rather, active seekers of solutions to problems'.[19] As a normal baby naturally wants to walk, so young children want to solve problems if we give them the tools.

Reading and writing have always been considered two of the basic skills taught in the primary years and most children find one or the other, or both, present long-standing difficulties hampering their learning in all areas of the curriculum. Infant teachers rightly feel a need to concentrate on these skills (together with number), but study of the past can motivate children to want to read, particularly as 7 to 8 year olds outgrow picture reading and one-sentence explanations of their own pictures. More highly-illustrated history books are being published, and 8 to 9 year olds feel very proud when they have read one book from cover to cover and even read it to other children. In reviewing materials for Philip and Tacey, Gerald Haigh writes, 'It is my experience that beginner readers like very small books, perhaps because they are less formidable in appearance.'[20] Young children learn a great deal from writing about a visit to a stately home, completing a composition by filling in word gaps, making sequence lines, family trees and other diagrammatic work. Below is an account of a visit to Croxteth Hall, a stately home in Liverpool, by 'Julie', a 6 year old from Lawrence Road Infants School, Wavertree.

Throughout the school years, as teachers we are trying to help our pupils to become thinking individuals. There has been a tendency for infant teachers to believe that too much 'thinking' was not good for young children. In the words of Julius Caesar, 'Yond Cassius has a lean and hungry look; He thinks too much: such men are dangerous. . . . He reads much; he is a great observer and he looks quite through the deeds of men' (*Julius Caesar*, Act 1, Scene 2). This feeling is reflected by young children; when asked whether she had enjoyed her work with

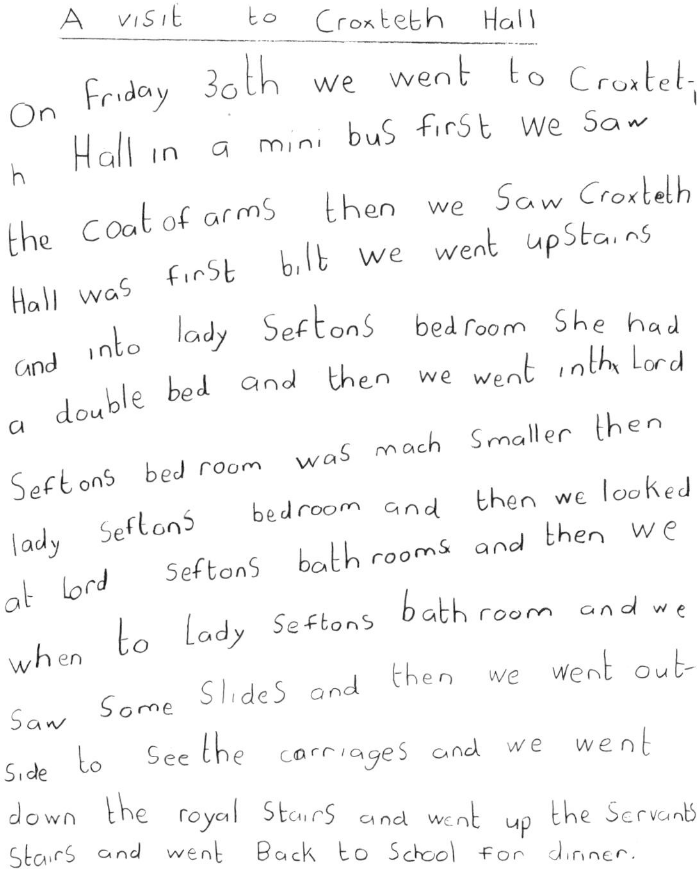

A visit to Croxteth Hall

On Friday 30th we went to Croxteth Hall in a mini bus first we saw the coat of arms then we saw Croxteth Hall was first bilt we went upstairs and into lady Seftons bedroom She had a double bed and then we went inth Lord Seftons bed room was mach Smaller then lady Seftons bedroom and then we looked at lord Seftons bath rooms and then we when to lady Seftons bath room and we Saw Some Slides and then we went outSide to See the carriages and we went down the royal Stairs and went up the Servants Stairs and went Back to School for dinner.

Figure 3.4 *Julie's account of our visit to Croxteth Hall*

me, a bright 6 year old said, holding her head with her hands 'It has been hard, thinking so much – you have worn my brain out'! Yet we need to bring children up to be thoughtful and critical of events around them 'looking quite through the deeds of men'. Peter Bryant and Margaret Donaldson think that some kind of logical thinking begins in children much sooner than has been conventionally believed in the light of Piaget's experiments. Peter Bryant also believes that a young child cannot reason easily because his memory is not normally exercised and he forgets the knowledge which helps him to reason.[21] Children learn to remember by repetition and reinforcement on the part of the teacher. Learning to sequence the four seasons helps children to place historical postcards in time order and to tell or write a story of events in the right order to make sense. Children, who saw relationships between historical characters and events in my tests, found thinking about the answers easier. Thus one boy of 9 sequenced the 'armour' postcards by relating armour to the Tower of London and Hampton Court Palace, both places he had visited and where he had seen armour. Hampton Court was connected with Henry VIII and therefore he could date the picture of the Tudor armour. Celia and Johan Modgil write, 'Time, like place, is constructed little by little and involves the elaboration of a system of relations.'[22] Thus children learn by teachers helping their stumbling efforts to see relationships between things.

Many psychologists have studied the processes of children's learning and how these change as children grow older. They have indicated in general terms that children learn some facts by association with other facts, but that they also learn by seeing situations as wholes. For example, in a story such as Goldilocks and the Three Bears they learn by association and meticulously repeat the detailed patterned sequence – 'Who has been eating my porridge? Who has been sitting in my chair?' and 'Who has been sleeping in my bed?' – but they also learn by grasping the shape of the story as a whole and thus being able to fill in gaps and even to anticipate details as the story develops. Yet the usefulness to teachers of educational psychology is limited because much of it has been carried out with individual children or in small group settings away from schools and classrooms. Also their language is technical and has not been 'translated' into everyday language which we can understand and relate to normal classroom activities. Teachers can learn from some of their findings and disagreements, but at 'the chalk face' they tend to work from experience and intuition and to try to help children to learn in their own way and at their own very varied paces.

But ultimately we all know that there are no rigid 'rules' about learning, that learning depends on *ad hoc* opportunities presented in the classroom each day and that among young children it is 'untidy' and inconsistent, yet in accordance with a general pattern of growth.

Notes

1. Aslett, G. (1987) *Using farm links with primary and middle schools*. MEd Dissertation, Cambridge Institute of Education. See pp. 11–13 of this book.

2. 'Peterloo' is the name given to the occasion in 1819 when 11 people were killed and 40 injured when soldiers rode into a large crowd listening to Henry Hunt's speech calling for an MP for Manchester. Peterloo has been compared with the battlefield of Waterloo.

3. Blyth, J. E. (1982) *History in Primary Schools*, pp. 44–6 and 65–72. Maidenhead: McGraw-Hill; Best, A. M. (1945) *Story-Telling: Notes for Teachers of History in the Junior School*. Historical Association Leaflet No. 13. Jayne Woodhouse and Viv Wilson write about role play on pp. 58–60 of this book.

4. Sylva, K. and Lunt, I. (1982) *Child Development: a First Course*, p. 124. Oxford: Blackwell.

5. Fontana, D. (ed.) (1984) *The Education of the Young Child*, p. 5. Oxford: Blackwell.

6. This point is also made in a study of 6 to 7 year olds by Bennett, N. *et al.* (1984) *The Quality of Pupil Learning Experiences*, p. 32. New Jersey: Lawrence Erlbaum Associates.

7. Harlen, W. (1985) *Teaching and Learning Primary Science*, pp. 124–6, 134, 142–5, 178–9. London: Harper and Row.

8. Words used by Dr Colin Conner in a discussion at Cambridge Institute of Education, October 1986.

9. Lally, J. and West, J. (1981) *The Child's Awareness of the Past: Teacher's Guide*, pp. 26–7. Hereford and Worcester: County History Advisory Committee.

10. Tough, J. (1984) 'How young children develop

and use language', p. 70, in Fontana, D. (ed.) (1984) *The Education of the Young Child.* Oxford: Blackwell.

11. Ibid., p. 74. Joan Tough directed the Schools Council *Communication Skills in Early Childhood Project*, 1971–76.

12. Sylva, K. and Lunt, I. (1982) op. cit., p. 129.

13. Ibid., p. 139.

14. 'The power of negative thinking', *Times Educational Supplement*, 21 September 1984.

15. Blyth, J. E. (1985) 'Sequence and time sense with 5 to 9 year olds', *Times Educational Supplement*, 29 November 1985.

16. Collicott, S. L. (1982) 'Families are History', *Child Education*, May 1982, talks of each child having a 'History Book'.

17. Collicott, S. L. (1979) 'Out and About', *Child Education*, July 1979; West, M. (1982) 'Kingswood', pp. 101–2, in Blyth, J. E. (1982) *History in Primary Schools.* Maidenhead: McGraw-Hill.

18. Sylva, K. and Lunt, I. (1982) op. cit., p. 95.

19. Fontana, D. (ed.) (1980) op. cit., p. 43.

20. 'A for Activities', *Times Educational Supplement*, 2 May 1986.

21. Bryant, P. (1974) *Perception and Understanding in Young Children.* London: Methuen.

22. Modgil, C. and S. (1984) 'The development of thinking and reasoning', p. 28, in Fontana, D. (ed.) (1984) *The Education of the Young Child.* Oxford: Blackwell.

4 What part of the past?

The past can figure in the curriculum for the 5 to 7 age range as part of other topics. It can also form the basis of such topics in the 7 to 9 age range but is often taught best then as a separate subject.

Teachers of children aged 7 to 9 or even 5 to 7 can thus plan a broad framework of curriculum, specifying positive historical content, provided that their planning is flexible enough to pursue ideas which particularly interest children as they arise. Rather than specifying particular periods, personalities and dates suitable for a year, I shall discuss resources and ways of presenting historical material and show how they can represent various aspects of the past. In most cases, teaching young children through artefacts, family and oral history, is teaching history backwards, from the known present to the more distant past of the late nineteenth century. This should be extended in the 7 to 9 age range by teaching the past in depth patches on whatever period a teacher has particular and appropriate knowledge suitable for developing basic historical concepts. This work should be linked to that taught from the age of 5 by constant use of a simple time-line largely devoid of actual dates (see p. 6). I shall therefore approach content (what part of the past?) through the following:

1 Artefacts — most suitable
2 Family history — for the
3 Oral history — 5 to 7 age range
4 Topics in British and local history analysed from the point of view of:
  (a) Evidence
  (b) Power — Most
  (c) Empathy — suitable
  (d) Sequence and change in a local study — for the 7 to 9
  (e) Interdependence of disciplines — age range

1 Artefacts

A family friend of long ago put her hat on the teacher's desk in an infant classroom and asked the children to draw it, label it and, if possible, write something about it. One child drew this 'object' with the label – 'Miss Ugley's hat' (my friend's name being Miss Utley!) So in the 1930s the 'object lesson' of the Edwardian school was still being used for children to observe, draw and question. In this case it was a contemporary piece of clothing, but it might well have been an older object which my friend had at home. In that case it would have been an artefact or old object used in the past, whether near or far. Although the purpose of the object lesson was not to help children to understand the past, it had the same aim as the use of artefacts today, in that it encouraged close observation, enquiry and discussion. Teachers now ask children to observe the artefact, handle it and answer the questions 'What is it?', 'How was it made?', 'Who made it?', 'What was it used for?' and, perhaps 'Can you guess when it was made?' This should lead to peer group discussion, drawing, writing, modelling, and discussion in the class as a whole. An artefact is an object made by the hand of man, and therefore the term does not apply to natural formations such as caves and rocks.

The regular use of historical artefacts tends to limit the part of the past studied in detail to the last hundred years unless recourse is had to museums and antique shops and showrooms. This is a very good beginning for 5 to 7 year olds learning about the past and involves sequencing of objects (putting in date order) on quite a substantial scale. It could well start a scheme of work throughout the primary school, treating the study of history in 'a regressive' way, beginning with the present and completing the work with prehistoric times in the fourth year. This view has been advocated by Michael Pollard in *History for Juniors*,[1] though he would not go back beyond about 1700. This approach also tends to limit the study of the past to social, domestic and local history, topics such as schools, children, toys, domestic chores, houses and the occasional old map and letter, often reflecting personal domestic happenings. In recent years, the Second World War has been popular as ration books, identity cards and gas masks have been recovered from desks and drawers. Coins of all ages are also easily handled. There is much good in this, although one would want to see a broader fare offered to younger children by the age of 9.

There has been a tendency throughout the primary school to think that the use of artefacts as a means of providing evidence for children to reach conclusions is the only way to teach the past. It is one of many ways and children easily tire of similar artefacts from the last hundred years. This very practical approach can edge out the study of people in

the past, and also places, other than the immediate locality.

This popularity may have evolved over the last few years as a result of help being given by some excellent publications, such as the Longman series, *Into the Past*, by Sallie Purkis, starting with the year 1900. From research I have recently undertaken in London schools, it appears to be a mistake for teachers to think that children of 9 use artefacts more competently than 6 year olds.[2] This particular method of approach, requiring little previous knowledge or memory retention, may be done better by some children of 6 than older children.

I shall consider what historical content can be taught to 5 to 9 year olds through the study of artefacts in four sections – children, domestic life, buildings, and maps and letters. Teachers are advised to study artefacts in these categories in order to gain an in-depth view of one particular area of life.

Children

(a) *Children at school*

This is an excellent topic; all children can compare their own schooling with that of their ancestors. Following the Education Act of 1870 setting up large numbers of Board Schools, voluntary schools were established to respond to their challenge. Therefore, by 1970 many schools were celebrating their centenaries with well-documented projects, often involving the whole school, using written evidence (logbooks) and artefacts for display.[3] There are now also several established school museums for children to visit and from which to gain information. Other general museums also include a room set aside as an Edwardian classroom complete with dual desks, teacher's high desk, books, rulers, canes, slates, abacuses and dumb-bells (see Figure 4.1). Some teachers' centres have kits of such materials and instructions about drill to lend to teachers for use in their own lessons. An example of this is Merton Teachers' Centre in Morden, London.

Figure 4.1 *An Edwardian classroom, Sudbury Hall Museum (Derbyshire Museum Service)*

(b) *Children at leisure*

A second area related to children might well be that covering Victorian/Edwardian children at home and on holiday (see Figure 4.2). This could include objects found in upper-class nurseries, such as spinning tops and whips, dolls' houses and their furniture, rocking horses, high chairs, music boxes, teddy bears, dolls, pinafores worn to protect clothes, story books, samplers, alphabet bricks and toy artefacts, sailor suits, straw hats and frilly dresses.[4] Much help can be gained from Bethnal Green Museum of Childhood (London) where a large collection of toys and costumes are exhibited. Even the catalogues and booklets which can be obtained by post are a tremendous help. The teacher should have plenty of background information available to make the artefacts come alive.

Portrayals of children in the Victorian period by Charles Dickens,[5] Charles Kingsley and Frances Hodgson Burnett are excellent sources for selected short reading passages, and can also be used for telling a serial-type story. There is also some valuable literature about Victorian children to be obtained from local organisations.[6] Molly Harrison's small books on children in different centuries are based on exhibits in the Geffrye Museum and are a constant practical help when teaching about artefacts relevant to children.[7] If artefacts alone are used, the actual life and feelings of children may be lost and too much emphasis put on 'how things work'. Therefore, reference to literature is strongly recommended.

Figure 4.2 *Shrimping in 1913 (BBC Hulton Picture Library)*

Domestic life

This category introduces children to adults in history and extends into the daily lives of different types of people, on a wider scale than just the last hundred years. Genuine or reproduced archaeological finds which throw light on the social life of prehistoric man, the Celts, Romans, Vikings and Saxons can be included. One group of 7 year olds I worked with recently in a London school derived most of their understanding of evidence of the Celts from postcards and pictures of exhibits in the British Museum. This work, and one visit to the British Museum gave a very good idea of what can be learnt from artefacts such as torcs, helmets and golden drinking vessels, even though the children were unable to handle them.

During the last hundred years, hardware such as washing tubs, wooden mangles, possers, brass pans for jam-making, and carpet-sweepers, have increasingly become 'by-gones', but examples which can be found are often tough and may be used by children in the right conditions. Soft materials can be found more easily and much can be gained from admiring lace-work, embroidery, samplers (as far back as the seventeenth century) (Figure 4.3) and items of clothing. Furniture and clocks are less easily found and handled by young children, yet one piece of small furniture, such as an embroidered stool, can be the origin of many avenues of discovery. Above all, as *Into the Past* has so ably shown, old photographs are a rich source of evidence, teaching children close observation and stimulating imagination.[8]

Buildings

When young children have looked at their counterparts in the past, both at school and at home, they should be encouraged to study larger artefacts such as the outside of smaller houses or one room inside a larger house.

Figure 4.3 *Seventeenth-century sampler (Fitzwilliam Museum, Cambridge)*

Thus an understanding of people of different periods and classes in society, in their domestic settings, can be gained. Such a study leads back from the Victorian town or terraced house to a Regency house, a Tudor half-timbered home, a fortified manor house and a castle.[9] Ruined buildings should be avoided as they require more effort of the imagination to envisage as a whole than a more or less complete building. It is worthwhile for a school to join the National Trust as this organisation has good educational facilities for teachers to arrange visits suitable for such young children. It is usually more productive for teachers to prepare, organise and guide their children rather than rely on the information of official guides less experienced with

young children. When arranging visits one must remember to relate the period of the building to a time-line in school. An important warning is that teachers get tired sooner than young children!

Maps and letters

Much written material in document form is obviously unsuitable for 5 to 9 year olds, but personal letters and old maps prove very attractive artefacts, in spite of their calligraphical difficulties. Letters from children to parents when at boarding school, from grandparents to children and those sent by friends to each other are most suitable artefacts. Town maps of the sixteenth and seventeenth century, such as those drawn by John Speed, are concerned with a sufficiently small area to be appreciated, especially if the map is of the local town. This provides a happy link between time and place for younger children and is a good way of teaching routes, names of streets and directions painlessly. Most libraries and archive deposits have very clear original old maps and can often supply good copies.[10]

The uses to which these artefacts can be put should be planned carefully, not only to ensure that sufficient artefacts are at hand, but also so that they can be worked on in a concentrated way to depict one topic at a specific time. This is likely to be within the last one hundred years. The artefacts should be related to a time-line and children should always do some recording work after their observation, handling and discussion. Study of artefacts should also be enriched by pictures, photographs, books and information supplied by the teacher on the same topic. The period from about 700 to 1855 AD is difficult to study by using artefacts except spasmodically.

2 Family history

The history of a family, whether that of the child, the teacher, a local celebrity or the royal family is closely associated with artefacts. Old objects, particularly small ones, have been owned and used by families. Those brought to school usually belong to the child's family and therefore the period of the past studies goes back 60 to 100 years, if one is lucky. As in the case of artefacts, family history can of course become repetitive and boring if studied throughout the four years of 5 to 9 schooling. It should be carefully placed in a scheme of work in the earlier years and linked with artefacts. It is also a regressive approach to the past as children are likely to know more about their grandparents than their great-grandparents.

During the last 20 years, tracing one's ancestors has become a fascinating pursuit for leisured and not so leisured adults, who have a natural curiosity to find out more about themselves through their ancestors.[11] Why have I got a quick temper? Why are my relations so mean? Why am I timid and fail to take up opportunities in life? Why do I have a mania for travel? Thus knowledge of one's ancestors can form excuses for our guilty consciences! Such people often agree to talk to young children about themselves and their family.

The 7 to 9 year old child can move from his own family to more famous families well-documented by records such as letters, diaries, inventories (lists of possessions attached to a will), census returns and parliamentary papers. (More detail will be given later in this section of the chapter on particular families and sources of information.) Teachers can gain enough information from one good book on most of these famous families so that young children may be introduced to periods before 1800 through the microcosm of one family.

Difficulties have been encountered in the early years of studying families; these have made some teachers doubt the effective use of family history. Many children do not have traditional family backgrounds, for example those with single parents and those whose fathers are in another country owing to immigration laws. On these occasions children can use well-documented historical characters if teachers accumulate a few appropriate sources for these emergencies. It is often wise to get younger children to work in pairs on one child's family if more resources are available for that family than another. This type of work trains children to make cautious inferences from slender evidence, a skill developed by historians. The use of family history can be discussed under five headings: your own family, a local family, the royal family, a family house and famous families of the past.

Your own family

Taking an example of an average 6 year old, the family is likely to be British, to have lived in one place for three generations (i.e. for the last 60 years), to have more than one child in one generation and to have relations living not far away. Information may be gained about great-grandparents from grandparents, which would extend the period of the past to about ninety years. Children from multicultural backgrounds who study their own families will provide opportunity of insights for the whole class into international history. The sequence of events in the child's 6 years may be recorded on a short horizontal or vertical sequence line divided into years 1 to 6.[12] The beginnings of a family tree may be made for three generations using single words (such as Mum, Dad, Granny) and writing these in prepared boxes.[13] Information about the three/four generations can be collected, using artefacts, drawings and stories, though the teacher has to be aware that some of these are 'tall stories' from over-imaginative children. These may be illustrated by photographs of the people themselves and from holiday post-cards sent to the child by members of the family. Thus a record of the family can be built up in an exercise book called 'My family'.

A local family

The work with 6 year olds might lead to the study of a well-known family that has lived in the locality for several generations. This family would have to be researched by the teacher and feelers put out to members of the family for permission and sources of information. Local and family history societies are often very helpful with this sort of work, especially with very old, established families. Thus Staffordshire children might study the Wedgwood family, Huntingdon children the Cromwell family and Manchester children the Prince family.[14] Family history in one area may also be studied from gravestones which is a good introduction to the usefulness of dates.[15] This also applies to brasses and family statues inside churches. Obviously, much detailed preparation must be done on the family by the teacher.

The royal family

During my recent research, I was surprised to find that young children do not know the relationships of the present royal family, in spite of the strong influence of the media. Several of my research children were unaware that the Duke of Edinburgh (Prince Philip) was married to the Queen or that the Queen had four children. Resources are easy to find for obvious reasons and children are delighted to bring in pictures. The royal family has the advantage of being well documented and can be traced back to Queen Victoria (1837–1901) and even George I (1714–27). Topics such as the Coronation, the Silver Jubilee and Royal Weddings, or a timely royal birth or tour, can form a central theme through which the family is studied. This may be done at the time of the event, for example the television programme about the Queen's work in the Second World War, or fitted regularly into the scheme of work to link onto other types of family history study.[16]

A family house

This type of work depends upon the availability of a local house, whether a cottage or a stately home. An outstanding example of the former is 15 Castle Hill, Lancaster, built in 1729 and used as the family home of a craftsman. Guide books for properties usually provide adequate information and do not hesitate to elaborate with relish on the 'black sheep' of the family. I have worked with 6 year olds on Lord Sefton's family (1880–1980) of Croxteth Hall, Liverpool and 9 year olds on the Catholic Norris family (1500–1700) of Speke Hall, Liverpool.[17] The Berkleys of Berkley Castle, Gloucestershire, Bess, Countess of Shrewsbury of Hardwick Hall[18] and the Spencers of Althorp, Northamptonshire (the family of the Princess of Wales) also provide delightful family subjects. These studies are made more relevant if visits to parts of the houses can be arranged, but much can be accomplished from pictures in books, slides and filmstrips as well as Elizabethan music on record. As mentioned earlier in this chapter a building can be used both for work or artefacts, for family history or a combination of both.

Famous families of the past

The stronghold of the 'here and now' has to be resisted and efforts must be made by teachers to venture out from the local and intimate family into new places and periods. Some families do not always have their houses still standing and therefore study of a family building may have to be omitted. Easily accessible material has been written about the famous families mentioned here. *Family History Patches* is a series published by Nelson in the late 1970s. *The Stonors* of Stonor Park in Oxfordshire describes a fifteenth-century gentry family. The *Lloyds* represents a seventeenth-century Quaker family. The *Steels* depicts a twentieth-century family. These small books are well illustrated with contemporary pictures, family trees (Figure 4.4), extracts from sources (to be used by the teacher if necessary) and activities for children. Many 8 to 9 year olds could read them

for themselves. The Pastons are a gentry family of the sixteenth and seventeenth centuries living at Paston on the coast of Norfolk; the main source of information on them is a collection of family letters.[19] The Verney Memoirs of the Civil War provide evidence of a gentry family divided against itself with members on both sides in the Civil War.[20] More obvious examples from the twentieth century include the Churchill family, and the Kennedy family in the USA. The family study could also encompass a Scottish clan or African tribe, both being extended families. Many children in schools today are familiar with this kind of family structure.

Learning about one's own and other people's families is of perennial interest to most of us, perhaps as a form of gossip. It is not of only antiquarian interest; scholarly academics have made it a special branch of historical study.[21] From the point of view of children aged 5 to 7, they can understand their own families, the royal family and family and wedding photographs, as being nearer to them and their own day-to-day interests. The local family, a building and family combined, and famous families of the past are more suitable topics for children aged 7 to 9. The whole subject of

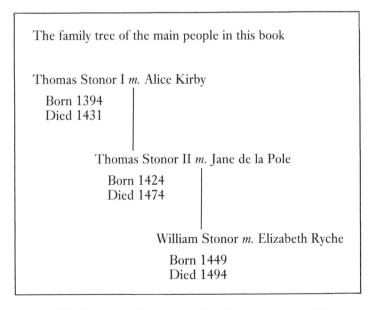

The family tree of the main people in this book

Thomas Stonor I *m.* Alice Kirby

    Born 1394
    Died 1431

           Thomas Stonor II *m.* Jane de la Pole

        Born 1424
        Died 1474

               William Stonor *m.* Elizabeth Ryche

            Born 1449
            Died 1494

Figure 4.4 *The Stonor family tree from* The Stonors *by P. J. Jefferies, Nelson*

family history 'has important implications for interdisciplinary work and for the relationship of the school to parents and the community at large . . .'[22] From the late 1960s onwards it has been used in both primary and secondary schools, particularly successfully by Brendan Murphy of St Cuthbert's Primary School, Wigan, with mainly older junior children.[23] This work is so fascinating for the teacher that care must be taken for it not to dominate all 'topic' and 'environmental study' time in all zones from 5 to 11. Family history covers any period of the past for which there are accessible records.

3 Oral history

Oral history may be interpreted as the evidence gained about the past from the spoken word, originally one person telling another about his past. This handing on of tradition and information in story form has taken place from time immemorial as story-telling,[24] but has not been used systematically in schools. This type of conversation is frequently tape-recorded, even by the child concerned and replayed when recapitulation is needed. Due to the work of historians at Essex and Kent

Universities, it has become a recognised and respectable form of historical enquiry.[25] It should be used more systematically by teachers of young children who are just learning to write and read and whose minds are quicker than their reading and writing skills. This applies particularly to the less able who think sensibly and well but cannot give a coherent explanation of their thoughts without help. Figure 4.5 shows how a 6 year old can benefit from oral and family history. This approach is closely linked to artefacts and family history and is good training in listening skills if the content has to be retold. It is also an offshoot of the familiar 'story-time' when children listen to the teacher telling a story. In this case, a story is told by an older person, relating his ordinary or extraordinary experiences during the last 50 to 90 years. The best known teacher to use oral history seriously is Sallie Purkis whose series *Into the Past* has become a best-seller (see p. 41 and Chapter 5, pp. 55–7. To date, 12 slim volumes have been published. They are concerned with ordinary lives in the twentieth century and are full of black and white photographs with a well-spaced, clear text, highlighting questions and suggesting activities for children.

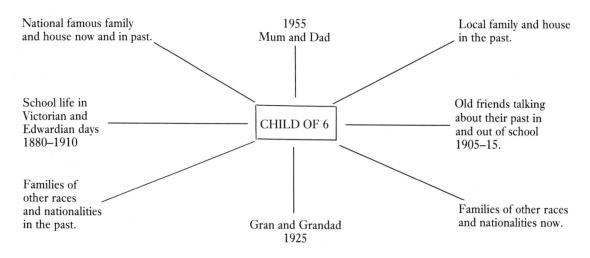

Oral and family history helps to 'decentre' the young child and widen horizons

| National famous family and house now and in past. | 1955 Mum and Dad | Local family and house in the past. |

School life in Victorian and Edwardian days 1880–1910 — CHILD OF 6 — Old friends talking about their past in and out of school 1905–15.

Families of other races and nationalities in the past.

Gran and Grandad 1925

Families of other races and nationalities now.

Figure 4.5 *A child of 6 – oral and family history*

We shall consider the topics available through oral history – all during the twentieth century – in relation to the light thrown on life at home, life at school and college, specialised occupations and other countries.

Life at home

Since women tend to outlive men, information about the domestic and working lives of women outside the home is likely to go back further than that about many other activities.

It is unlikely that one speaker could hold the attention of a whole class of 30 children and therefore it is better to divide the class into three groups and invite three older people to talk about their lives at home many years ago. These visitors are often able to bring artefacts, letters, diaries and books to illustrate their conversation. It gives a broader view of society if people from different types of background agree to talk, especially if they can form a panel at the end to compare their ways of life.[26] Sallie Purkis's two books, *At Home in 1900* and *At Home in the 1930s*, in the series mentioned above, are useful as supplementary material for these comparison sessions.

Life at school and college

This sort of discussion might be initiated by the teacher talking about her school and college days and her own teaching experiences. Visitors could be invited after this session; they should include a retired teacher as well as other people. Different types of school should be studied: primary and secondary, day and boarding, comprehensive, grammar and secondary modern, and perhaps colleges of education and their counterparts. It might be possible to extend this work to the experiences of students at universities and in other forms of higher education. Recently I came across the Oxford memories of a woman undergraduate of 1909–1913.[27] They throw light on the position of women in a bastion of male privilege in the early part of the century and include amusing incidents and reflections.

Specialised occupations

Oral history is not only a source for social life, but also a valuable means of finding out what occupations in existence during the last hundred years are still pursued today. Thus history can become 'social studies' or 'citizenship'.

The service jobs of policeman/woman, bus conductor (few of them now), shopkeeper, farmer, factory worker and owner, window-cleaner, train driver and many others, can be detailed by older people talking to children and outlining a day in their lives, their holidays (paid and unpaid) and wages.

Different forms of religion might be part of the syllabus and an Anglican clergyman, other representative Christians, a Rabbi and Moslem Imam, and members of other sects could be invited into the school. Reference should be made to the headmaster/mistress as to how far this is acceptable.

The topic War Work in the Second World War might involve stories from air raid wardens, a member of the Forces, land girls and fire watchers. A 'now and then' project could also be undertaken for the sake of comparison; for example, the life of a farmer of 1930 would be very different from that of a farmer in 1987.

Other countries

Although I favour concentration on British history in the 5 to 9 years of schooling, a scheme of work could include links with places other than Britain through oral history. This depends to a large extent on whether the teacher can find suitable subjects in the locality. It is more realistic to use natives of the countries chosen but many British people have lived and travelled abroad and could talk about the way of life in a European country, USA or the Third World. Care must be taken here to invite a visitor who has good command of English and knows how to talk to young children. Parents who have originated from other countries could make an invaluable contribution here. It would also be valuable to use a map to place the country involved, and also to try to concentrate on one country or type of occupation instead of several which can be confusing.

The use of older people coming into school must be systematised, built into the scheme of work, prepared thoroughly and followed up by the children in their own activities and recording of work. The same visitors might be used for several years and this type of work needs practice on the part of the subjects and the children. Care should be taken not to use the same speakers in other years of the primary school. The skilled work of interviewing and tape-recording by children in a one-to-one situation will be discussed later in this book. Much useful advice is given by Paul Thompson in the Model Questions section at the back of his book.[28] In answer to the question 'What part of the past do 5 to 9 age children study?' through oral history, the answer is the local past of this century and possibly a small part of the late nineteenth century. The concluding words of Paul Thompson's book are worth relating to young children: 'Oral history gives history back to the people in their own words. And in giving a past, it also helps them towards a future of their own making.'[29]

4 Topics in British and local history

The above aspects of content apply equally to the whole age range, but at 7 years of age children are to be encouraged to venture into pastures new and study certain topics from different parts of the past in depth.

Before deciding upon a scheme of work for children aged 7 to 9, many factors must be considered. In the first place the needs of children aged 9 to 11 and beyond must fit in with the scheme, to avoid repetition of topics. Other factors are teachers' interests and expertise, the local environment and other resources available, such as books, maps and funds to allow visits. The need for mixed-ability teaching should also be considered.

Teachers should avoid the temptation to let schools television decide topics as these programmes are unlikely to fit the school scheme. If possible, it is better to video-record the likely programmes for future use and introduce them as illustrations of your own theme, regardless of what the notes accompanying the programmes say (Chapter 6, pp. 84–5).

All schemes from the earliest age should refer to a sequence/time-line which enables topics to be studied according to school decisions instead of exact chronology (see p. 6). This enforced use of time-lines encourages children to develop a sense of sequence and time more quickly than keeping to chronology.[30] In devising a scheme of work, one hopes that two topics would be covered in depth each year and therefore six or more should be offered for choice over the two years.

The HMI document *Education 5 to 9* carefully avoids the word 'history' as being too academic for children of this age. 'Learning about People' is the title given to the section on history, although history is more than this. 'It would be pretentious to label work of this kind, done with 5 and 6 year olds as social studies, geography or history, but some of the skills, ideas and knowledge associated with these subjects were in some of the work.'[31] Let us call it 'history' and have more of these skills, ideas and knowledge and avoid 'the fragmented and superficial nature of what children are doing'. The 'lack of appreciation of suitable work that could be done with younger children . . .'[32] stems from not 'calling a spade a spade'. In the words of Paul Noble, a primary headmaster, 'a discussion of historical studies in the primary school and the formulation of appropriate curricular policies, can hardly be facilitated by a reluctance to employ the correct terminology. History, after all, is history, is history'.[33]

It would be impossible to discuss all the historical topics suitable for the 7 to 9 age range and therefore I am using five sets of topics loosely related to certain historical ideas which are needed by the age of 9. They are evidence, power, empathy, sequence and change in a local study, and the interdependence of discipline through a topic involving history, geography, social studies and literature.

Evidence

Perhaps the most important skill of the historian is to check information by collecting different types of evidence, some reliable and some unreliable, to prove truth or otherwise. From recent research[34] I have found that children of the age under discussion are quite competent handlers of evidence. The results of testing 37 children in London schools have shown that children draw valid conclusions about school life from artefacts of Edwardian schools but they do not so easily understand sequence (time), change/difference or power. Therefore, topics in the past which have left more artefacts than written remains are suitable content for study. Prehistoric times (including the Stone Age and Bronze Age), the Celts, Romans, Saxons and Vikings offer many archaeological remains which can be found in museums, at archaeological digs and in illustrations in books. These periods should be recorded on the time-line, without dates, in the correct sequence. At the other end of chronology the Victorians are also a favourite topic on account of the artefacts left. Whether the early or later period is studied at 7 to 9, or later, is immaterial as long as it is not repeated in other years and is placed on the time-line.

Power

Children may not understand the concept of power but they certainly understand conflict, fighting, quarrelling, hatred and war at a very

Figure 4.6 *A scene from the Bayeux Tapestry (with permission of the town of Bayeux)*

early age. I was pleasantly surprised when administering my test for power (Chapter 3, p. 26) how much the children appreciated the power of a handful of soldiers over the crowds in St Peter's Square, Manchester, on 16 August, 1819; some children even related the power over the soldiers to Parliament in London and the fact that Manchester at that time did not have an MP (before the Reform Act of 1832). Suitable topics, such as the Norman Conquest in 1066, provide clear evidence of the power of William of Normandy in invading England, his desire to teach Harold a lesson and to strengthen himself as Duke of Normandy against the King of France, his enemy (France was not ruled by one King in 1066). (Resources for this work will be discussed in Chapter 5, pp. 51 and 72.) This topic can also include evidence from the contemporary embroidery, the Bayeux Tapestry (Figure 4.6). It also stimulates empathy towards both William, Harold, the Norman soldiers away from home and the Saxons being invaded. Another, less obvious topic for the understanding of power, is a study of castles, which in themselves represent physical power. The obvious question arises as to why such strong buildings were needed. If a developmental study of castles is made from Norman times (Tower of London), to Edward I's castles in Wales (1307–27), to Tudor fortified manor houses and then to fortified stately homes (often still looking like castles), change/difference as well as sequence/time can be taught.

Empathy

'Empathy . . . is a quality which enables us to know what it is like to be in somebody else's shoes.'[35] It is easier to be 'in the shoes' of people in our own time, but in an in-depth study of one narrow topic this can also be done for periods of the past. For example, the Elizabethan Court is a delightful topic, full of colourful personalities, houses, masques, music and romance; it is well supplied with appropriate illustrations and literature. What was it like to be a woman 'at the top' in a court dominated by clever and high-spirited men and influenced by warring religious factions? What was it like to be banned from the Court, as was the Earl of Essex? The English Civil War (1642–9) has left its scars on most areas of England and Wales and is again a study of easy empathy. Charles I's life was at stake, Prince Rupert's military reputation was at stake, individual families were rent apart (for example, the Verney family in Buckinghamshire) and 'the common man'[36] was being killed for causes he did not understand. How different from the fight against Fascism – or was it? Even more remote but a good topic for empathetic study is monks and monasteries. Who were monks? Why did men (and women) choose this life in such numbers? What did they do all day? Did they quarrel living together all the time? Were the rules of the monastic orders just and helpful? Teachers must make a special effort to discuss power and empathy in relation to the topics being studied and not presume that children will make their own links.

Sequence and change in a local study

An in-depth study of a narrow topic may be complimented by a detailed study of one village, town or suburb throughout its history. This teaches change/difference as well as sequence/time and involves visits, study of plans and simple maps and can involve personalities of the past. It is obviously best to study one's own town (if small enough), but resources can be collected to study another town even if there is no opportunity to visit it. Certain outstanding examples come to mind. Lavenham in Suffolk, calling itself 'the finest medieval town in England' (see Figure 4.7) has undulating fairy-like streets of crooked, medieval houses supported by wooden beams, a Guildhall, market cross and large church (expressing the prosperity of the medieval wool trade). Other less spectacular but worthwhile small towns to study are Ludlow (Shropshire), Helmsley (North Yorkshire), Nantwich (Cheshire), Prestbury (near

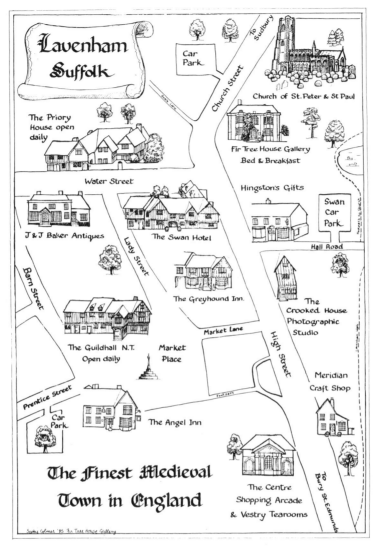

Figure 4.7 *Medieval Lavenham (with permission of the Lavenham Publicity Group)*

Macclesfield), Stamford (Lincolnshire), Wells (Somerset) and Rye (Sussex).

Interdependence of disciplines

Decisions as to whether, when and how to integrate the social subjects have to be made as part of school policy. Some people advocate combined work in the 5 to 9 age range, separate disciplines in the 8 to 10 age range and environmental studies taught as part of history and geography in the fourth year. Many teachers call all this work environmental studies or topic throughout the school without seeing the need to define the title more specifically. Some terms they teach history, geography, environmental studies or a broader topic or centre of interest, including other disciplines when appropriate. More will be said about this in Chapter 5 (pp. 70–2), but many experienced teachers believe that 'it is up to the teacher to integrate'[37] without detailed advice being given in a scheme of work. Care should be taken to give balance to the subject disciplines involved when planning integrated schemes and to guard against the domination of a topic by one discipline year after year as the teacher's interest dictates.

It is difficult to teach historical skills and attitudes in any developmental way in a combined course. Local work lends itself to a combination of history and geography, and a study of life in the eighteenth and nineteenth centuries could well introduce literature from novels of the period. (Jane Austen, Charles Dickens, George Eliot, Benjamin Disraeli and Mrs Gaskell are good examples.) Integrated work will remain suspect to historians until more relevant historical information is used by teachers and pupils and a well thought out topic is prepared incorporating skills and concepts belonging to each discipline in more or less equal quantity.[38] Examples of such topics might be 'Discoverers of the New World', 'the American West', and 'London Poor in the Nineteenth Century'. Elizabeth Bouchier writes of her work with infants using an historical approach to the unlikely topic of 'Milk':

MILK – NOW AND THEN – WITH A RECEPTION CLASS

This project was undertaken as part of the PGCE at Manchester Polytechnic. Students were required to consider the contribution of their degree subject to teaching in the primary school and to undertake relevant work with the children. As a history graduate I decided to incorporate a historical perspective into my topic work.

Throughout the teaching practice, my class of 4 and 5 year olds worked on the theme of Food and in the final week we concentrated on the subject of Milk. The school was situated opposite a dairy and the children therefore had first-hand experience of seeing milk tankers and floats arrive and depart. In addition, a shopping visit earlier in the practice had involved one group looking at the different containers for milk available in the supermarket. Having worked on present-day methods of collecting and delivering milk, I gradually began to direct the children's thoughts towards the past through informal discussions when the class was gathered together. My method of introducing this to the children in a meaningful way was to talk about 'long ago' and to describe it as 'not when I was a little girl, not when my mummy was a little girl, but when my grandma was a little girl'. The focus of this project was a visit from my own grandmother who talked to the children about the milkman of her childhood and brought several old objects for the children to handle and discuss. At the end of this session I told the children a story, using the various artefacts as visual aids and the children then drew the artefacts and talked about their pictures to both myself and my grandmother. The work involved a number of approaches which can be listed as follows:

(a) *Use of visual sources* These included a large, colourful picture of a milkman of the past with his hand-cart complete with large churn and smaller milk cans. Two children were pictured buying milk and the milkman was measuring it out into their jug. Pictures used earlier of modern milkmen and their floats were on display for reference during the session.

As the children were very young I tried to develop an awareness of the past by focusing their attention on the differences and similarities between 'then and now'.[39] Inspired by the picture we thought about the sort of clothes the milkmen wore, how they transported and sold their milk and what the milk was delivered in.

(b) *Oral history* This involved a visit from my grandmother who talked about how milk was taken from the cow by hand, carried in milk churns by horse and cart, delivered by a milkman who pushed a handcart and filled her own jug from his large churn. In order to emphasise the similarities and differences between the two periods I asked the children to tell my grandmother all that we had learnt about milk production today and she, in response to their comments, told them what had happened when she was young.

(c) *Use of artefacts* These included a full-sized old milk churn, an old milk can, a half pint measure used to measure the milk from the churn to the customer's jug, a milking stool and the jug my grandmother used to buy her milk in. The use of real objects which the children could see and touch helped make her words much more meaningful.

(d) *Storytelling* In order to reinforce the children's learning and to 'bring history alive', I wove the various artefacts and information into story form. The story was inspired by a small milk can which was dented and had a bent handle. The retired milkman from whom I had borrowed the can told me that the dent was the result of an accident with a bicycle. I therefore told the story of 'How the milk can got its dent'.

(e) *Recording and evaluation* The children were asked to draw pictures of anything we had discussed relating to the past. The artefacts were left on display so that they could draw these if they wished.

It is obviously very difficult to accurately assess the children's understanding of the historical concepts I was trying to introduce. They worked very enthusiastically and thoroughly enjoyed listening to my grandmother and handling the artefacts. The children's drawings and comments about their pictures (which I recorded) gave some indication of the extent to which they succeeded in acquiring a sense of the past. The story method of imparting information clearly caught many children's imagination and fifteen of them drew pictures representing part of the story and including some of the artefacts. I was concerned to discover whether the children had realised that the story was set in another period and in cases where this was unclear I asked the child 'Is this now or when grandma was a little girl?' I was surprised by the number of children who immediately responded that it was in the past. Five other children drew the artefacts, simply naming them or describing their use to me. Alex clearly differentiated between 'then' and 'now', drawing several artefacts and asking, 'Can we do another picture of things we use today?' He then drew a milk bottle.

By using my main theme of Food as a starting point it was easy when planning to add history to the list of curriculum areas. It meant that the children were introduced to history through a topic that they had already worked on and enabled me successfully to introduce a young reception class to the past.

Elizabeth Bouchier, PGCE Student at Manchester Polytechnic.

With the growing emphasis on the specialist/consultant in the 'early years' it should be easier for checks to be made on integrated schemes of work. There is a danger of too much emphasis on history (or any other discipline) if there is *only* a specialist/consultant with a degree in history. Too many consultants looking after the integrated schemes might lead to chaos without the steadying influence of a wise headteacher! Lesley Abbott,[40] of Manchester Polytechnic, views the HMI document *Curriculum 5 to 16*[41]

47

as adding a complication when it refers to 'Broad Areas of Experience' for the specialist/consultant to be concerned with. She sees this role as a daunting one and integrated schemes of work will depend upon its success.

I have omitted stories of the past which is a usual way for the past to be taught to younger children. Stories link artefacts, family and oral history and patch studies of earlier history. All stories narrate a sequence of what happened, to whom, and when, even if 'when' is 'once upon a time'. Stories must be made up about the artefacts, about family life and the life of other people and the life of a Roman soldier or an Elizabethan courtier. Everyday objects are little inspiration without people and these people must have 'lived, moved and had their being'. Whatever scheme is adopted it should take at least one element from the past before 1000 AD, between 1000 and 1900, during the twentieth century and a local study, as part of the scheme. It is easier to use British history as much as possible because of the more readily available essential resources. Celia Macey gives help with resources for multi-cultural work in Chapter 6 (pp. 89–91). Each school should work out a policy towards other cultures, depending on the needs of their particular children. This is such an important consideration that all specialist co-ordinators should be involved, particularly the co-ordinator of religious education. Margaret Donaldson thinks that a young child can only 'gain a measure of control over his own thinking' if he 'learns to move beyond the bounds of human sense' which is 'unnatural in the sense that it does not happen spontaneously'. This movement 'is the product of long ages of culture', of which the past is an essential part. She goes on to say 'But in another sense the movement is not unnatural at all – it is merely the fostering of latent power.'[42] It matters little which part of our past is identified with our culture, for it all is. But 'familiarity breeds contempt' and young children need to study a variety of topics from the past, and be encouraged to make the first step towards distinguishing the old from the older.

Notes

1. Pollard, M. (1973) *History for Juniors*. London: Evans.
2. Blyth, J. E. (1985) *Understanding the Past – Children 5–9*. Typed report in the Library of Froebel College, Roehampton.
3. DES (1970) Education Act. London: HMSO; Tyson, J. C. (ed.) (1969) *Popular Education 1700–1870*. Newcastle-upon-Tyne: Department of Education.
4. Buck, A. M. (1959) *Children's Costume*, The Gallery of English Costume, Platt Hall, Manchester; also The Museum of Childhood, The Judges' Lodgings, Lancaster.
5. *David Copperfield, The Old Curiosity Shop, Oliver Twist, The Water Babies, Little Lord Fauntleroy*. Also see McChord Crothers, S. (1925) *The Children of Dickens*. New York: Scribners.
6. Hocking, S. K. (1968) *Her Benny*. Neston, South Wirral: Gallery Press; Francis, C. (ed.) (1969) *Orphan Annie*. Manchester Branch Historical Association (archive unit); *Voices from the Past, 1890–1940*, see Chapter 6, 'Children at Work', p. 80 of this book.
7. Harrison, M. (1967) *Children in History*. Cheltenham: Hulton. (One book for each century.)
8. Lansdell, A. (1983) *Wedding Fashions, 1860–1980, History in Camera*. Aylesbury: Shire Publications; Marshall, P. (1985) *Holidays, The Camera as Witness*; (1986) *Houses and Homes, The Camera as Witness*. London: Macdonald. Shearer, E. (1982) *Victorian Children at Turton Tower*. Blackburn Recreation Department.
10. An introduction should be given to the skills of map-reading. See Blyth, J. (1984) *Place and Time with Children Five to Nine*, pp. 58–64. Beckenham: Croom Helm.
11. Burns, N. (1962) *Family Tree*. London: Faber; Pine, L. G. (1966) *Tracing Your Ancestors*. London: Evans; Iredale, D. (1970) *Your Family Tree*. Aylesbury: Shire Publications; Totton, E. (1980) *My Family Tree Book*. London: Bell & Hyman; Exley, E. and H. (1975) *Grandmas and Grandpas* (13 editions). Watford: Exley Publications Ltd.
12. For examples see Blyth, J. E. (1982) *History in Primary Schools*, p. 118. Maidenhead: McGraw-Hill and Blyth, J. E. (1984) op. cit., p. 67.
13. Blyth, J. E. (1984) op. cit., p. 70.
14. Rosser, M. (ed.) (1972) *The Princes of Loom Street*. Manchester Branch Historical Association (archive unit).
15. Lindley, K. (1972) *Graves and Graveyards*. London: Routledge and Kegan Paul.
16. Marshall, P. (1985) *The Royal Family*, Camera as Witness. London: Macdonald, is an excellent source for this purpose.
17. Blyth, J. E. (1984) op. cit., pp. 125–42; Cook, M. and Blyth, J. E. (eds) (1970) *A Tudor House: Speke Hall and the Norris Family 1500–1700*. The Liverpool

Teachers' Archives Study Group, Liverpool Education Committee.

18. Plowden, A. (1972) *Mistress of Hardwick*. London: BBC Publications; Reeves, M. (1984) *The Elizabethan Country House*. Harlow: Longman.

19. Ball, A. H. R. (ed.) (1949) *Selections from the Paston Letters*. London: Harrap.

20. Verney, Sir Harry (ed.) (1968) *The Verneys of Claydon*. Oxford: Pergamon Press; Slater, M. (1984) *Family Life in the Seventeenth Century, The Verneys of Claydon House*. London: Routledge and Kegan Paul.

21. Ariès, Philippe (1960) *Centuries of Childhood*. Harmondsworth: Penguin; Stone, L. (1977) *Family, Sex and Marriage*. Harmondsworth: Penguin; Houlbrooke, R. A. (1984) *The English Family 1450–1700*. Harlow: Longman.

22. Steel, D. J. and Taylor, L. (1973) *Family History in Schools* (Preface). Chichester: Phillimore.

23. Murphy, B. J. (1971) 'History through the Family I' and Steel, D. J. and Taylor, L. (1971) 'History through the Family II' both in *Teaching History*, May, Vol. II, No. 5, Historical Association.

24. Evans, George Ewart (1970) *Where Beards Wag All: the Relevance of the Oral Tradition*. London: Faber.

25. Thompson, P. (1978) *The Voice of the Past*. Oxford: Oxford University Press.

26. A good comparison of 'upstairs downstairs' life before 1900 is given in Wagstaff, S. (1978) *Two Victorian Families* London: A & C Black.

27. Odlum, Dr Doris (1983) 'Some Oxford Memories' in St Hilda's College Report and Chronicle 1983–4, pp. 53–5.

28. Thompson, P. (1978) op. cit., pp. 243–52.

29. Ibid., p. 226.

30. Blyth, J. E. (1984) op. cit., Figures 3:10–3:11, pp. 68–9.

31. DES (1982) *Education 5 to 9*, p. 28. London: HMSO.

32. Ibid., p. 81.

33. Noble, P. (1985) 'Seeking for a sense of direction', *Times Educational Supplement Extra*, 12 April 1985, p. 36.

34. Blyth, J. E. (1985) op. cit.

35. Blyth, A. *et al.* (1975) *Place Time and Society 8–13 – An Introduction*. From the School Curriculum Development Committee.

36. Wedgwood, C. V. (1957) *The Common Man in the Great Civil War*. Leicester: Leicester University Press.

37. Taylor, D., Adviser in Primary Education (1984) in *Environmental Studies in the Primary School*, a Scottish National In-Service Course at Aberdeen College of Education, p. 13.

38. Fines, J. (1970) *The History Teacher and Other Disciplines*, TH28 Historical Association.

39. Low-Beer, A. and Blyth, J. E. (1983) *Teaching History to Younger Children*, TH52 Historical Association, p. 28. Other examples may be found in Blyth, J. E. (1984) op. cit., pp. 35–41.

40. Abbott, L. (1986) 'The Role of the Specialist/Consultant in the Early Years', *Education in the Early Years*, *Greater Manchester Primary Contact*, Special Issue No. 5.

41. DES (1985) *Curriculum 5–16*. London: HMSO.

42. Donaldson, M. (1978) *Children's Minds*, p. 123. London: Fontana.

5 Teaching techniques

J. S. Bruner's philosophy is that all disciplines can be taught successfully to all ages of children if the appropriate teaching strategies are used. This presents a particular challenge to teachers of young children in relation to the past. The DES publication, *History in the Primary and Secondary Years*,[1] pays specific attention to the years 5 to 8, thus approving the need for young children to study the past. In this publication 'stories and myths' and 'artefacts and activities' are highlighted as suitable techniques for the teacher. With a growing emphasis on the need to 'match' work to each child, to seek progression of skills as the child moves up the primary school and to stretch the more able adequately, there is a real need for teachers to discuss 'how' they are presenting material and what specific activities the children are to undertake.

My recent research points to two prerequisites of the teacher of young children in this area of the curriculum. One is the need for her to have basic knowledge of the part of the past being taught. Many teachers in primary schools have university degrees which involve the study of history, but this does not necessarily mean that they know enough about a particular topic taught in school. Very often the enthusiastic non-historian who has developed a particular interest in a topic provides more interesting material for children. The open-ended method of topic teaching for half

a term involving a visit to an historic site or museum requires more detailed knowledge of a period of the past than teaching it for GCSE. Bright 8 to 9 year olds are keen to know 'how things work' and have time and energy to be full of questions which few adults could answer. In this age of teaching skills and concepts in which 'content' tends to get a bad name, there is a temptation for teachers of 5 to 9 year olds to use disjointed pieces of information which 'turn up' in everyday life. This approach may be adequate for a social studies topic of 'the milkman's round' or 'the policeman's beat', but it is disastrous when teaching about medieval armour or eighteenth-century coffee houses. It is better to know thoroughly about two historical topics and build up this knowledge as the years go by rather than dip into any areas of the past requested by pupils in a superficial manner. Children enjoy the accurate details of what real people were actually doing as portrayed by contemporary sources.

The second prerequisite for the teacher is the ability and desire to plan her work with children well ahead and structure and resource it so as to provide helpful activities related to the topic. This involves good discipline, a balance between oral teaching and child activity, good timing and the right pace, so as to give time for adequate discussion and yet not be boring. In my research, I found that the children taught by the most highly organised teacher learnt more about the past. An example is that of a highly organised teacher most successfully studying the Norman Conquest with her mixed ability 7 year olds. She prepared in detail, had board work ready before the lesson started and was in complete control of how the lesson proceeded. She recapitulated by questioning the main points of the previous lesson and linked the new lesson on to it. Her oral exposition was clear and stimulating and she used appropriate resources.[2] Most of her lessons, of one hour's duration, were divided into two, three or four independent parts; for example, on one occasion she used oral exposition, a filmstrip of the Bayeux Tapestry and provided relevant activity as a third part. The children were excited by the story of the Battle of Hastings and wondered who was going to win, William or Harold. One boy said he knew who won, but, he added with relish, 'I'm not telling anyone who won'. Thus each lesson was 'the next exciting instalment'.

Far more detailed help with teaching techniques, and bearing in mind that a variety of approaches is more stimulating than a well worn method, see Figure 5.1. The two overriding considerations affecting all the other methods are sequence/time and topics. A sense of time must pervade all teaching of the past and be introduced into all other methods. Most schools use 'topic', 'environmental studies' or 'project' as an umbrella title for studies involving the past, including history, as well as other areas of the humanities, such as geography. The six groups of techniques all involve sequence and time and are methods used in 'topic'.

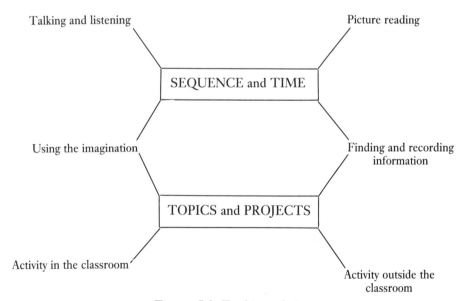

Figure 5.1 *Teaching techniques*

Sequence and time

'There is no reason why children, by the time they leave primary schools, should not have acquired a chronological structure that enables them to use such terms as "Stone Age", "Greek and Roman", "Medieval", "Tudor", "Victorian" and "recent" correctly.'[3] This considered judgement by the history HMI reflects current views of both historians and infant specialists. Therefore we must find ways of teaching sequence and time which are interesting and which 'work'. This will help children to put names of historical periods in correct sequence.

The interest in the concept of sequence has

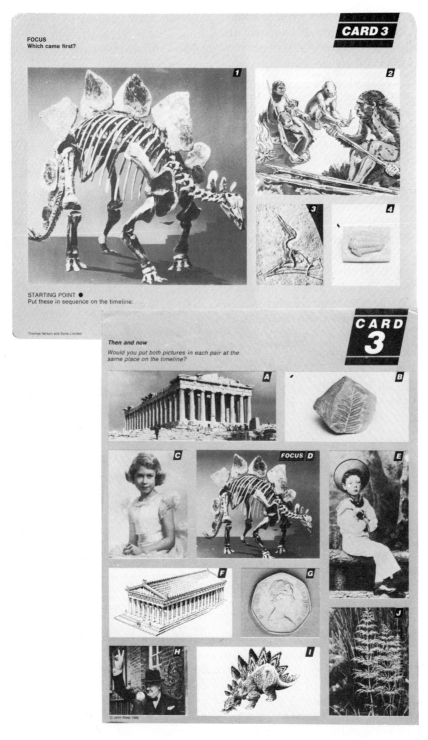

Figure 5.2 *'Then and Now' from* Time Line *by John West, Nelson*

developed over the last ten years and several research workers in the primary field are investigating how their own classes can comprehend sequence, then time (V. A. Bone, Chapter 2, p. 11). An interesting development has taken place in the last year as geographers and scientists are concerned with other types of sequence (G. Aslett, Chapter 2, p. 11). Thus it may be possible to view sequence as a general concept applicable to all learning. Training in one area of the curriculum may be transferred to another. An obvious example is the sequencing of events needed when children are listening to a story (see Chapter 3, pp. 26–7). This interest is leading publishers to produce materials to help teachers.[4]

It is certain that this surge of interest in sequencing owes its origin to John West whose work has already been mentioned (see Chapter 2, p. 8). He created ten picture sequence cards on various familiar topics which children identified and then put in historical sequence (Figure 5.2). If a class is divided into groups handling different cards they can eventually sequence all the cards and relate them to their time-line round the classroom wall. They can then put copies of the pictures in the correct place on the time-line. If a shelf is conveniently placed underneath the time-line, artefacts, replicas and models of the pictures will further reinforce the concept of sequence. The same piece of classroom wall may be used for different time spans according to the period studied. It could represent the nine years of a child's life, or, for example, the 'century' of 1837–1937. Young children do not readily understand duration or dates, though the birth of Christ (significant for BC/AD understanding), 1066, 1588, 1837 and 1939 are convenient 'pegs'. Children's conception of time is helped by mathematical calculations, writing, completing sequence/time-lines and ongoing discussion.

My own research on sequence in five London schools (1983–5) was based on John West's work. The aims were to find out whether 6 to 9 year olds could put postcards of the past in correct time order, what reasons

Figure 5.3 *Roman soldier (Grosvenor Museum, Chester)*

they had for this order and whether they had any awareness of a sense of period. The random topics of travel, houses, armour and costume were chosen because of accessibility to postcards/pictures interesting to this age-group. The methods used were for the child (in a one-to-one situation) to be given a jumbled 'pack' of 2, 3, 4 or 5 cards (in turn) which they were asked to put in correct sequence. When this was done they were asked for reasons for this order and allowed to change the order before the Sequence Chart was completed (one for each set of six children in each school). This was an attempt to discourage children from guessing. They were finally told the correct order and the names and dates of the postcards. No direct requests for information or 'correct answers' were given before each part of the test was attempted. A child, a pair of children or a group of children could carry out this exercise without the teacher if the correct sequence was accessible after the task was completed.

The children as a whole found the 'armour' set of cards the most difficult (Figure 5.3).

The result showed that the concept of sequence was beginning to be grasped and could be well developed before the end of primary schooling. I also tested the same children for their understanding of the concepts of evidence, change and power; they found sequence nearly as difficult as power. Success depended upon four factors related to the children. One was intelligence and command of language; this helped the children to give their reasons for sequencing clearly and fairly quickly which was necessary in an oral test being tape-recorded. A second factor was motivation and concentration which was high for all the children. They relished the 'test' situation unfamiliar to many of them, and were keen to alter their first effort at sequencing after discussion. A third factor was imagination, observation of details in the cards and confidence to make successful guesses. The 9 year olds scored well on this third factor because of their greater maturity. A final qualification for success was the ability to see the past as a whole. If the children related the sequence postcards to each other and saw travel, houses, armour and costume in their own developing situation, they had this ability. So they had to recognise a postcard as not only 'not like now' and therefore somewhere in the past, but also in relation to other postcards in the same category. Several children used other factors such as houses, weapons and landscape to help them to place the postcards correctly. The children's abilities were dependent on how they had been taught over the years. Children experienced in time-lines and used to probing questions in discussion did well in the test, as did children who were content with grey areas of right and wrong.

The straight, simple sequence or time-line used vertically or horizontally[5] has much to commend it as it can be made by the teacher quickly and by children when they can use a ruler firmly. But there are other approaches to time.[6] One is a time 'train' on a railway track marked out for periods of time, the lines being used for names of important events. Another is a time clock of a day, a week, a month, a year or a century, with a hand pointing to the moment under discussion.[7] A time chart shows dates at the top with plenty of space for events underneath connected with one 'line of development'. A picture time chart includes space, dates and pictures, preferably made by the children.

Throughout her teaching of the past, the teacher should use vocabulary and explain words such as 'century', 'manor' and 'stone circle'. She must persuade her children to use the correct terms for historical objects, events, pieces of clothing and parts of buildings. An awareness of period can be given by children knowing that 'nobles' do not live in nineteenth-century England and that 'cloaks' are not worn by men today. In the next section I shall be discussing 'Talking and listening', and more will be said at that stage about the use of the past in teaching language to young children.

Talking and listening

Story-time should be an institution in the infant school as a short period when all practical activity ceases and children gather round their teacher and listen to words of interest, fun and wisdom. It is the privilege of all students to sit at the feet of their teacher imbibing the experience of life in preparation for the future. If the story is well told or well read you should be able to hear a pin drop. Why not a true story of the past?

Understanding the adult world through reading or handling old objects is difficult for young children and perhaps the only way to tell children about 'heroes and villains'[8] and to draw lessons from the past, is to tell a straight story. After the telling,[9] suitable probing questions can lead to discussion when teacher and children are talking and listening in turn. John West's research, in which many stories were told by teachers, led him to evolve appropriate questions related to the stories.[10] These should be prepared beforehand to lead children to extended thinking. For example, the story of Richard II, aged 14, and his part in the Peasants' Revolt raises many empathetic and ethical questions which children can come to appreciate when put by the teacher. Was Richard brave? Why did he make promises to the peasants and then withdraw them? Was he cunning, at the age of 14, or fearful of what the nobility would do to him if he gave in to the rebels? Richard died in his thirties at Pontefract Castle; was this deserved and how did he die? Children are thus brought to understand the complexities of human beings.

A story is also a good way to present a series of exciting events leading to a crisis, such as the Battle of Hastings. The sequencing technique discussed earlier is needed when children listen to a new story as events in the wrong position do not make sense. Few young children seem able to retell a narrative story without leaving something out and a story of the past is a good exercise in understanding sequence. *Telling Tales Together*[11] is a video showing adults telling stories from different cultures translated into English and minority languages. It also shows children sharing stories, some of which are from the past of different cultures. This project by the Cadmean Trust has been found to be a unifying experience in multicultural schools.

Much work has been done most effectively on oral and family history with young children, using the memories of old people in studying the last 60 to 80 years. Tapes are kept by many schools to form a library for future generations of children.[12] But story-telling and oral history can be overworked in the later stages of the junior school at the expense of documentary work and the reading of information books for projects. It is best used in the 5 to 9 age range. More will be said about listening to radio broadcasts and resources for oral history in Chapter 6.

Sallie Purkis writes as follows:

ORAL HISTORY IN THE CLASS-ROOM

One of the most positive ways of introducing the past to young children is by inviting someone into the classroom to talk about the time they have lived through. If the person chosen is known for their ability to communicate effectively with this age group (an experienced granny or grandad would be ideal to start with), then the chances are that they will bring the past alive in a vivid and interesting way. As the average life-span is now much longer than it was even 30 years ago, most of us know plenty of people over 60 and probably a good number of octagenarians. Many have time on their hands and welcome the opportunities for contact with children and an invitation to go out. To gain the maximum benefit from such a visit however, it is worth the teacher taking time to think about a number of factors in preparation for such a visit.

TOPIC OR RESPONDENT? WHICH TO CHOOSE FIRST?

Whether the teacher first chooses a topic about the past or a respondent who can talk about the past is something of a chicken and egg situation. The important thing to remember is that oral history is about recruiting *eyewitnesses* to talk about their *own* experiences, experiences, of course, that are likely to interest young children. First draw up a list of possible respondents or ways of finding them. The school may already have contacts with old people in the area and invite them to school to see the Christmas entertainment or send them a parcel at Harvest Festival time. If not, there may be some sheltered housing or an Over-Sixties lunch club near the school. Once you have a list of names, take time to find out a little about their lives, where they lived and what work they did before retirement. A group of pensioners, for example, who have lived near the school all their lives would be an ideal group to talk about some of the changes they had seen in the neighbourhood; some may even have been pupils at the school or one nearby that could be visited. If, on the other hand, your pensioners have only recently moved to the area, it would be more appropriate to focus on a general theme: a period of time like 'Fifty Years Ago', 'Living through the 1930s' or a common experience like 'Childhood' to which everyone could contribute even if they had been brought up in other parts of the United Kingdom, or abroad. Even a very broad theme like 'Time', 'The Past', or 'Change' can also be resourced and enriched by an older person's reminiscences. When matching a respondent with a topic, remind yourself that to be authentic, oral history must be the firsthand evidence of someone who was actually where they say they were at a particular point in time. Beware of the pitfall of asking someone to talk about the London Blitz who can convincingly argue that they know all about it because they have seen newsreel films or read books, but who were actually living in rural East Anglia at the time.

PREPARING FOR A SCHOOL VISIT

Having identified a suitable visitor, told them about the topic you wish them to talk about and made the necessary arrangements for them to come to school, you will need to think of ways of preparing the children. Tell them a little bit about Mrs Green or whoever, where she lives now and how old she is. With all but the very youngest children, this could be an opportunity for a little work on 'time'. Time-lines for Mrs Green could be drawn alongside those for themselves and anyone else they can

think of. Practice with some historical vocabulary could also be initiated: then and now, past, present and future, 'before the war', decades, and how to measure concepts like 'long ago'. Ways of encouraging Mrs Green to talk about her experiences can be discussed, whether there might be some ways of 'jogging' her memory and even what questions the children would like to ask her. Don't be tempted, however to over-structure the actual encounter between Mrs Green and the children by giving them some rather stilted questions to read out. A rigid questionnaire might be appropriate for an adult researcher/historian but with primary school children it could inhibit the flow of a good narrative and frustrate the desired objective of bringing the past alive. Some teachers make a short 'tick list' to remind themselves of the potential of the interview. Memory joggers or prompts can be put in brackets. So if, for example, someone has been asked to talk about the time when they were a child, the following preparatory notes might be drawn up:

Who was in the family? (mother, father, grandparents, brothers, sisters).
Family home (place, description including facilities available, memories of family life).
Schooldays (place, size, teachers, lessons, friends).
Games played (indoors, outdoors, toys, friends).
Special events (Christmas, birthdays, outings, holidays).

TALK AS HISTORICAL EVIDENCE

The value of having a good story-teller in the classroom, with whose experiences the children can identify, cannot be over-emphasised. However, as part of an initiation into the discipline of history, the story must be seen by the children to be a true one. Its authenticity can be supported by other evidence, some supplied by the respondent herself, some by the teacher with the help of resources outside. The most likely additional pieces of evidence will be photographs, personal documents, working tools and other artefacts of the period. A touching description of a pensioner's visit to a classroom in Wales was given in Schools Council Working Paper 48 when an old miner showed children the medal he had won for bravery rescuing trapped miners, and let them touch his miner's lamp and helmet.

AFTER THE INTERVIEW

Oral history experiences can lead to productive follow-up work. The children can write about the visit and the things they remember about it. Younger ones can draw pictures both of the visitor and how they think she was when younger. If the interview has been recorded the teacher can transcribe extracts, perhaps displaying them beside the old photographs, artefacts or children's drawings. The time-line can be introduced again with extracts from the talk put into their correct time context. If the same questions can be put to someone 30 or 50 years younger than the first visitor then comparisons can be made between the experiences of the visitors and the children's own. The children can be helped to analyse the evidence by the teacher pointing them to the key conceptual areas of continuity and change, similarity and difference.

Best of all, however, is the creative opportunities this technique offers for transforming the talk into a piece of history in the form of a little booklet. With the help of the reprographic services of the local Teachers' Centre the class can produce a book with a title like *Fifty Years Ago, Our Past, In Grandma's Day* or something similar. Parents and friends would probably be prepared to pay a modest sum to offset the expense. When put on public display this kind of history is very popular as can be seen when old photographs are published in the local paper. The booklet or display will inevitably stimulate more reminiscence and the school will have a collection of resource material that may be suitable in other topics.

Sallie Purkis, Homerton College, Cambridge.[13]

Using the imagination

Story-telling stimulates the imagination and is not far removed from role play, drama and the use of historical fiction in the classroom. These teaching techniques introduce activity into a study of the past as well as being cheap and usually only needing homemade costumes as props in the 5 to 9 age range.

In a perceptive and historically-based article, Philip Jones,[14] a London primary teacher, puts forward an argument for widening the curriculum in history from a study of the locality and the practical present to a more distant past. He writes, 'dressing up and taking part weave a spell over even the youngest historians'. He coins a new phrase in 'temporal chauvinism', meaning that only the present is honoured. This has happened partly because history 'textbooks' are out of fashion and teachers have not had time to create appropriate resources for earlier times. He believes that 'history has rarely been more than tale-telling' and therefore one should capitalise on the good story by letting it lead to role play and drama. He advises schools to build up libraries of historical stories of different periods and cultures.

Role play is an activity which can be undertaken spontaneously in a small space by all age-groups. For many years the work of Dorothy Heathcote[15] has had a considerable influence on teachers, and her pupil, Ray Verrier, and his colleague, John Fines,[16] have

57

developed her work in the south of England. The aim was not only to teach children about the past but also to get them to empathise and feel as people of the past felt. There is also a moral tone attached to her work and which some feel is much needed in schools today. Teachers are advised to start with a story, or part story, involving people of the past, leading to discussion of the part played by different personalities. Then the children take on different roles and at first move about the room carrying out the physical actions of the story without words. This enables even shy children to participate. Finally, they use impromptu words in the jargon of the period, if possible, which children fall into quite easily. Documents can be acted out as well as stories and most archives' collections have documents relating to, for example, a meeting of the manor court or a meeting of William the Conqueror's commissioners with the shire court for the Domesday Survey of 1086.

Drama involving dressing up and scenery can be undertaken on special occasions (see S. Blakeway's work in Chapter 2, p. 13), but the teacher must beware of the children getting so concerned with their costumes that they forget their roles and the historical importance of them. Therefore a dramatic presentation is usually best undertaken as a whole-school project (if a small school) to make a special event in the life of the school and/or locality. For example, children from the village school at Blewbury in Oxfordshire undertook a pageant depicting nine hundred years of Blewbury life. More than one hundred 5 to 11 year olds were involved in July 1986. The Project was engineered by the headmistress and the photograph in the *Times Educational Supplement* is entitled 'History is alive and well'. As the pageant involved Normans to Victorians, Philip Jones would be satisfied by the spread of the period.[17] On the same lines and as an exceptional example, 75 8 to 9 year olds from St Mark's Middle School in Southampton re-enacted a 1566 Court Leet, adapted from original Court Leet documents.[18] Jayne Woodhouse and Viv Wilson explain the experiment here:

THE TUDOR COURT LEET OF 1566 AT SOUTHAMPTON COMMON

The use of drama role play to help children develop a deeper understanding of an historical period is an exciting and rewarding method of teaching history. This approach has been used with great success by Roger Day, County Drama Adviser for Wiltshire. Over the last ten years, he has involved literally hundreds of children in storylines which have ranged from the trial of a notorious eighteenth-century highwayman to the visit of William the Conqueror at Old Sarum. As the climax of these projects, the children spend a whole day in role at an historic site, where the drama focuses on an authentic event from the past. In order to sustain such a level of commitment over a prolonged period, detailed classroom preparation is a vital part of the learning process.

During the summer term of 1986, we were involved with a local Southampton Middle School in a similar history and drama project for two classes of 8 and 9 year olds. Neither class teachers nor children had had any previous experience of working in this way. However, by the end of the project the interest and excitement shown by the children, together with the enthusiasm of the staff who took part, confirmed the value of this teaching method.

The focus of the project was the sixteenth-century Court Leet — the early civic court — of the City of Southampton. In choosing this particular event, we were guided by the existence of the original Court Leet site — the Cutthorn mound on Southampton Common — which was within walking distance of St Mark's School. Also the documentary evidence of cases tried during 1566

Figure 5.4 *A case is heard against a merchant accused of selling bad spices*

gave us authentic names, offences and punishments which formed the basis of much subsequent drama role play. Preparatory work in class concentrated on helping the children explore the details of everyday life in Southampton during the sixteenth century, from the varying viewpoints of the characters they would eventually assume. As a starting point, each child and teacher was given an authentic Tudor name, occupation and address in the city, adapted from local records. From this point teachers worked in role as a vital strategy in the ensuing drama work.

In the weeks leading up to the event on the Common, the children developed their own 'personal histories' as the citizens of Elizabethan Southampton. Drama sessions helped to deepen the children's sense of identification with their characters, as they created scenes of daily life in shops, streets and taverns. Documentary evidence gave us an indication of the types of contemporary domestic and civil disputes which were heard at the Court Leet. We aimed at creating similar incidents in our group work, without drawing directly from the primary sources. By the end of the project, the children were sufficiently confident in their roles to bring the knowledge and experience gained from their research and drama work to the new context of the Court Leet.

The final history and drama day began with children and adults dressed in Tudor costume walking to the Cutthorn mound, as their sixteenth-century predecessors would have done. Some had disputes to settle, others stood accused of offences whose outcome was as yet unknown, while many had come for the sport and entertainment which traditionally accompanied the more serious business of the Court.

On arrival they were greeted by the 'Mayor' in municipal robes and chain of office (Roger Day, who as an LEA Adviser had readily agreed to work with us). The company then processed to beat the bounds of the Court site, and afterwards dispersed to enjoy various games and sports of the period: skittles, bowls, tug-of-war, and archery and wrestling contests. Following an open-air feast, enlivened by entertainment including music and dancing, the jury was sworn in and the proceedings of the Court began.

None of the presentments made by the citizens had been formally prepared or rehearsed, but were drawn from the drama sessions held in school. The confidence with which the children approached the giving of evidence, and their ability to retain their historical identities throughout the day's events, along with great inventiveness in language use, were an indication of the effectiveness of the teaching project. For the children taking part, the experience was 'real', because they were presented with situations drawn from their previous experience, and because they could directly affect the outcome of the problems facing them, without knowing in advance what the results would be.

The majority of complaints brought by the children to the Court were domestic disputes rather than criminal offences. It was through the experience of examining issues such as the sale of bad beer, or underweight goods that their sense of involvement with the period was clearly demonstrated. Among the highlights of the Court hearing was the evidence given by Edward Sendys, the butcher (Andrew, aged 9) concerning the case against Sir Francis Dawtrey. Sir Francis had been accused of pasturing his cows on the Common without licence, but Sendys insisted he had seen a licence in Sir Francis' possession. On being challenged by the Mayor as to whether he could read, Sendys proceeded to demonstrate his ability to the Court by reading aloud from a book of sixteenth-century sermons! The case against Sir Francis was dismissed.

One of the major aims of history teaching in the primary school is to help children develop a sense of empathy with the individual men and women who make up our past. This project illustrates how a combination of history and drama, particularly when reinforced by an entire day's activity in role, is a most effective means of achieving this end.

Jayne Woodhouse and Viv Wilson, La Sainte Union College, Southampton.

On a larger scale, outside agencies are providing dramatic experiences for children brought to a stately home for a day's work. This not only relieves teachers of vast amounts of preparation, but the experience is also prepared more professionally by the bodies concerned. Clarke Hall at Wakefield is an LEA museum of seventeenth-century bygones which children visit to relive this period by dressing up and handling artefacts. Kentwell Hall owned by Patrick Philips at Long Melton, Suffolk, also provides 'Tudor days' each July for children to dress up and take on roles of different Tudor characters, mainly well-known ones connected with the Elizabethan Court. One year the theme was 'Kentwell 1535 – Henry VIII: Reformation'. The Young National Trust players tour schools enacting different periods of the past and the Heritage Education Trust has been set up to interest children in historic houses by role play and drama in the correct setting of the stately home.[19] Peter Thorogood has bought St Mary's, a fifteenth-century house in West Sussex, for public opening and also for schools to use for educational purposes. All these experiences are conducted in a relaxed manner and are unrehearsed by the children. Younger children usually feel the set play, either written by or for them, is inappropriate, as they find reading a play difficult and their memories are not retentive for 'learning lines'.

Children's imaginations can also be stirred by select parts of historical novels. Teachers familiar with the nineteenth-century novels of Charles Dickens, such as *Oliver Twist, David Copperfield* and *A Christmas Carol*, all involving children, may find an opportunity to illustrate their teaching from reference or quotation. But more historical fiction for junior age children has been published since 1950 and is concerned with 'long ago' times of legendary figures, Saxons and Vikings. I advise teachers of young children to use them for two purposes other than their own pleasure and enlargement of knowledge. One use is for illustration of a point by reading a paragraph or two of a certain book. For example, Cynthia Harnett's *The Woolpack*[20] has a detailed description of a medieval shepherd's home in Chapter 2, beginning 'It was a cosy little house of plastered timber and thatch . . .'. This could well be used for discussion, and even role play with the parts of the boys Nicholas and Hal being re-enacted. The other purpose is for the teacher to read the book in instalments in storytime. (More will be said about other historical novels in Chapter 6.) A recent pamphlet[21] by Vivienne Little and Trevor John is a mine of information for the teacher, although most of it applies to older children. There are, however, two interesting case studies of primary teachers using specific novels with 8 to 9 year olds. One is Kathleen Fidler's *The Boy with the Bronze Axe*[22] (Stone Age village life). The other study uses Henry Treece's *The Children's Crusade*[23] and Ronald Welch's *Knight Crusader*.[24] Both teachers give detailed step by step ways of using the books. Ann Low-Beer has written a useful article detailing particular historical novels she has found successful.[25]

Picture reading

So many of the teaching techniques suggested in this chapter depend upon pictorial representation for their success. Sequence cards and pictures for story-telling are in this category. As we found in Chapter 3, young children learn by 'reading' pictures. The example was given of the two street scenes I had used in tests. Yet many researchers and teachers have found young children not trained to read pictures in order to extract a story from them. Gill Aslett has found this in her picture reading for sequencing of the seasons. I also discovered this in all three of my tests which involved reading pictures. So far, little has been written to help teachers in picture reading, either in studying the past or in any other area of the curriculum. As so much pictorial representation is used in the lower part of the primary school this is a big omission in educational publishing. Robert Unwin[26] has written a detailed pamphlet on how to use historical pictures, but only a small part is devoted to young children.

The variety of pictures which can be used as a resource will be discussed in Chapter 6. Here I shall give detailed examples of how to use pictures from earlier periods of the past; a 1580 map of Chester, an eighteenth-century engraving of a sixteenth-century painting (*The Encampment of the English Forces near Portsmouth*), *Eliza Triumphans* a painting by Robert Peake about 1600 and W. F. Yeames' famous nineteenth-century depiction of a seventeenth-century child in a stressful situation, *And when did you last see your father?* More will be said in Chapter 6 about pre-Tudor illustrations, which involve photographs of museum artefacts and replicas and medieval scenes in manuscripts such as the Luttrell Psalter.

The map of Chester in 1580 (Braun's map of Chester c.1580, see below) is a good example of an early town plan to be found in other old walled towns such as York, Lincoln and Southampton. The River Dee encloses two sides of the town of Chester which should lead to questions about trade and Chester as

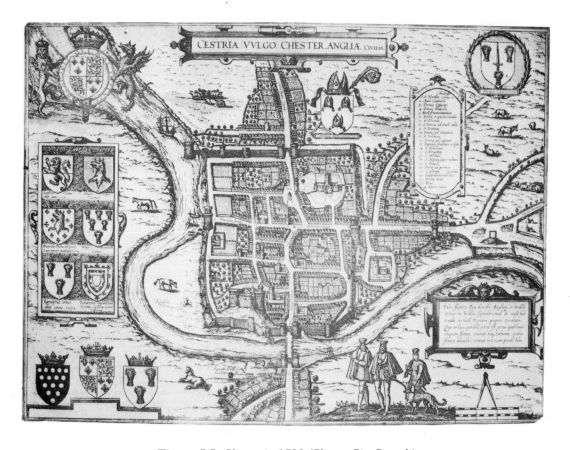

Figure 5.5 *Chester in 1580 (Chester City Records)*

an important port. Children should be asked to find the four gates of the city, old Dee Bridge, the cathedral (once a monastery), the castle, the walls, the many church spires and towers and the gardens of the small town houses. Chester's importance as a legionary fortress is shown by the straight roads. Why did Chester expand north and east? With help from an outline plan, older children could draw in the main streets, houses, churches and the four gates (with their towers). The Tudor gentlemen, animals and coats of arms add other talking points. Role play could involve Chester tradesmen (shoemakers, glove-makers, butchers, etc.) meeting at the High Cross (where the four roads meet) to talk about their work. Thus close observation, discussion, drawing and role play could develop from 'reading' this map.

The engraving of the sinking of the Tudor *Mary Rose* ship is a long picture (about 3 ft × 1 ft) which three children could use at the same time (see Figure 5.6). It is full of interesting activity, showing Henry VIII's fleet going out of Portsmouth to fight the French in 1545, the *Mary Rose* sinking, a gun tower, Southsea Castle, the tents of the soldiers and the walled town of Portsmouth. Even Henry VIII may be seen riding on his horse near Southsea Castle to give the *Mary Rose* a royal send off. This picture is so evocative that the children will be quick to point out people and things and ask questions themselves. The central event of the sinking of the *Mary Rose* and the drowned bodies of the soldiers and sailors in the sea are clearly visible. The majority of figures, including the king, are unaware of the tragedy but the soldiers near

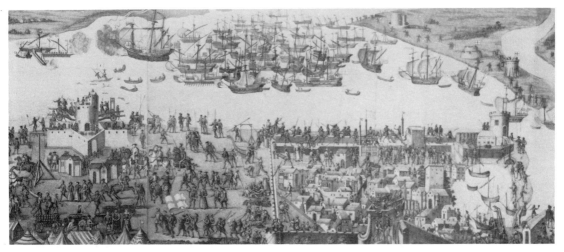

Figure 5.6 The Encampment of the English forces at Portsmouth 1545, *part of the Cowdry print obtainable from the City Museum and Art Gallery, Museum Road, Old Portsmouth PO1 2LJ*

the sea are not. Comparison can be made between this engraving and a modern atlas map showing the Isle of Wight in relation to Portsmouth. Thus children can observe clearly, discuss at length, draw ships, castles, Tudor figures and horses as well as try to find out more about the *Mary Rose*.

The two remaining pictures are on a smaller scale than either the map or the engraving. They are both suitable for very young children, even 4 to 5 year olds. *Eliza Triumphans*, or *The Procession of Queen Elizabeth I*, shows Elizabeth I progressing with her courtiers. I used this picture as a pre-test in four London schools with small groups of children. My test was called 'Picture Clues' and involved the

Figure 5.7 Eliza Triumphans *or* The Procession of Queen Elizabeth I *by Robert Peake the Elder c. 1600, Sherborne Castle, Cheap Street, Sherborne, Dorset DT9 3PY*

Figure 5.8 And when did you last see your father? *(Walker Art Gallery, Liverpool)*

children looking for clues about people, social life, costume, buildings and travel in the Tudor age. I asked questions about evidence (who was in the picture and what was happening?), change (how was Elizabeth I different from Elizabeth II?), power (who was the most important person in the picture and why?). The individual courtiers round the queen evoked considerable discussion; was the bald courtier at the front specially important and has one courtier got two left legs? This picture reading could well lead to finding out more about Tudor costume, the queen, Tudor buildings and social life.

The other, smaller picture seems to depict a small Royalist boy being questioned sternly by Cromwell's Puritan followers at the time of the Civil War as to where his father is – *And when did you last see your father?*[27] The painting evokes sympathy for the small boy, dressed in a pale blue satin suit (shades of Little Lord Fauntleroy?) attended by his weeping older sister, who is presumably next to be questioned. I used this picture with two groups of 4 to 5 year olds who had not studied the past beyond the difficult concept of Guy Fawkes and why he was executed. (We had just passed 5 November.) The central figure here is a

small boy of about 7 or 8; his loyalty to his father (and King Charles I) under pressure, may be held up as a good example. The glowering looks of the Puritan inquisitors, the clerk taking notes with a quill pen and the soldier preparing the boy's sister for her ordeal, all add pathos to the emotive scene. Observation and exchange of ideas about the people and objects contained in the painting are the most useful techniques to use, but it also provides a 'way in' for discussion of power in the Civil War period and how the struggle involved all families. Why did half the people of England want to fight their king, Charles I? Is it right to fight for 'freedom'? Obviously this picture can be used in different ways with 5 year olds and 9 year olds, perhaps in discussing loyalty to parents or understanding of war between people of the same country.

These four pictures need different approaches to the past but all require detailed observation. Two are concerned with spatial factors (map of Chester and Portsmouth panorama), two with particular historical crises (the sinking of the *Mary Rose* and the Civil War) and two with the concept of power (procession of Elizabeth I and the Civil War). All are delightful to use with young children who set about looking and thinking and asking questions enthusiastically.

Activity in the classroom

Many of the techniques discussed so far have involved young children's physical activity. This applies to using sequence cards, tape-recording old people and role play. Children are beginning to learn by 'concrete operations' during these years and are wanting to 'do' things in the classroom. How willing young children are to help the teacher with jobs after school if they are waiting for mum, dad or child-minder! I shall now take three 'concrete' activities to discuss in more detail. Model-making and picture making are two well-known activities. The handling of artefacts or replicas of them from museums, is becoming a most effective approach (see Chapter 2, pp. 17–19).

From time immemorial young children have enjoyed drawing and painting with crayons, painting sticks and paint. These pictures on paper of different sorts, or on 'detail' (or lining) paper if a brass is being rubbed, may be kept in a notebook, on large sheets of paper, or displayed as part of a frieze on the wall. They are usually original reconstructions and not 'copied' from elsewhere. The same sort of activity can take place with pictures cut out of old textbooks or magazines or even cut from intended published material.[28] Teachers should not be concerned that young children draw *their* idea of the past as it means that they are thinking about it. It is surprising how much children's drawings of Norman soldiers resemble those in the Bayeux Tapestry or in a medieval manuscript!

The use of small slide viewers by individuals, pairs or groups, has enabled children to look at many types of illustration, from a medieval monk to the trenches in the Second World War. This technique will be discussed further in Chapter 6 (see pp. 77–80). Yet children find it hard to show slides to their classmates even if they know a lot about both the slides and the other children. It is well worth training two children to show six slides (three each) to their peers, one working the projector and the other giving (or reading out) information. By the age of 9, they should be able to do this, including pointing out interesting features in the picture and even answering sensible questions from the other children. Initial embarrassment is the chief hurdle to overcome as I found in my work with 6 year olds,[29] but this type of exercise promotes a very useful life-skill.

Model-making in paper, cardboard, Plasticine, polystyrene or Lego bricks is part of the 'stock in trade' of 5 to 9 year olds and the more 'mess' the more enjoyable. Eight to 9 year olds can also make relief maps on strong bases for an environmental study involving the past. The creation of an historical model requires more detailed information than talking or writing about it. Much very useful advice has been given on techniques by experienced and well-qualified teachers.[30]

Using old objects has already been discussed in relation to research (Chapter 2, pp. 18–20), to ways of learning (Chapter 3, p. 28, and to content (Chapter 4, pp. 32–7), and it is always an effective method of enabling young children to see, handle and think about evidence of the past in a tangible form. John Davis, writes of his experiments.[31]

THE USE OF ARTEFACTS IN THE PRIMARY SCHOOL

It was a warm afternoon in May yet it could have been Christmas. Children working in small groups of three or four were selecting parcels from a large box and unwrapping them excitedly. Inside each parcel was an artefact and the purpose of the wrapping was to create an element of surprise, arouse interest and increase motivation. As it emerged from its covering, instant decisions had to be made about each object. How

Figure 5.9 *What does it say?*

should it be held? Which way up did it go? Could it be opened?

Earlier the class of lower juniors had been further stimulated by being told they were to play historical detectives and that once uncovered they should examine each object carefully looking for clues. To act as a framework for discussion, groups were given a work card containing a number of key questions. These included: What do you think the object is made of? What might it have been used for? Do you know how old it is? Would this object be used now?

As they talked, groups were encouraged to think about the shape, size, texture and composition of their artefact and to make sensible guesses in response to the questions asked. Often more spontaneous and revealing reactions can be produced if a group of children are placed in a room on their own and their conversation taped. De-

tailed sketches of the objects were done at this stage to encourage close observation. Initially, each group concentrated on one object, but as discussion developed, the others were passed around. This sharing of experience continued later when groups were asked to report on what they had discovered. It was important here for the teacher to assume the role of prompter and extender, making the children enlarge on their findings with questions like, how do you know? and what makes you think that?

The opportunity was also taken during these discussions to place the artefacts on a time-line. The main aim was to develop the children's sense of time by getting them to think about when the objects had first been used and then arranging them in some sequence of order. Actual details about the composition, uses, age and authenticity of the

Figure 5.10 *How does it work?*

artefacts were given to the children at this stage so they were able to make comparisons and see how their own efforts had matched up.

This information, in addition to their own findings, led the children into a further phase of study, using one of the objects they had examined as the basis for a wide range of cross-curricular activities. These allowed children to explore important historical concepts like then/now, similarity/difference, develop vital communication skills including researching, reading, writing and discussing as well as engage in many artistic and creative tasks. It also helped them appreciate that examining artefacts pushes the historian into further research. The detective work continues even when the actual object has been put down.

Using a glass pop bottle with a marble stopper as their starting point, some children went on to find out about glass-making and compared modern drinks containers with those of the past. Mathematical work involving tessellation and symmetry stemmed from an examination of a small piece of Roman mosaic while a spinning top led to activity on the changes in children's toys. Interviews with parents and grandparents enabled comparisons to be made over three generations.

To encourage feelings of empathy and thought about what it was like to live in the past, children were asked to choose one of the artefacts and make it the central feature of a story. They were asked to think about who might have used the object first, what they might have been wearing and what things they would have known about. One child wrote about a piece of pottery discovered after an air raid in World War Two while another used a candlestick in an eighteenth-century whodunnit. Such stories can easily lead to both role play and drama.

Children were given immediate feedback on what they were doing and completed tasks, mounted into a large display, illustrated the same methodical approach and enabled children to share easily the experience of other groups. Discussion at the beginning of each session revised what had been done previously, reinforced points which had emerged and produced suggestions for further extension.

Soon, children were wanting to make their own collections of historical objects. Weekends of scouring lofts and spare rooms produced items ranging from old medicine bottles to medals and coins. These were discussed, labelled and mounted into a display. One object of notable interest was a hand-carved wooden vase from Pitcairn Island. This not only aroused interest in the Mutiny on the Bounty story, but also resulted in a problem-solving task for the class working in groups. If you were set adrift in an eight metre boat like Captain Bligh and his supporters, children were asked, what ten items would you take with you given the choice?

With younger children, in the 4–7 age group, artefacts help to create an awareness of the past and begin the establishment of essential historical vocabulary. The accent here needs to be on class or group discussion in which the senses, especially sight and touch, are prominent. Tactile experience can be heightened by placing the objects in a 'feely' bag, and painting and drawing assist observation. At this level objects can also be used to stimulate class collections and displays and lead to simple time-lining and sequencing.

What appeals most to all children who use artefacts in the classroom is their immediacy. The thrill of being able to handle something of this kind in such a concrete and tangible way, knowing it has also been handled by someone in the past leaves a lasting impression. At a deeper level, it emphasises the interplay between evidence and the asking of questions and gives children some basic insight into the way in which the historian works, observing historical objects closely and through discussion and reasoning, making sensible deductions about them.

John Davis, Whitchurch County Primary School, Bristol.

Activity outside the classroom

At all stages of the years from 5 to 9, outside work should be planned so that by 9 children have visited a museum, one old building and undertaken a topic involving the near locality. If, in addition, they have become beginner archaeologists and found how 'below the ground' tells us about the past, so much the better. All these experiences involve preparation, a carefully planned time outside school and a thorough follow-up in the classroom. They are all concerned with evidence and 'how do we know?'

A good start for 6 year olds is a visit to part of the nearest museum. This could take a whole term with preparation and follow up. Museum Education Officers are trained to help teachers and often run courses for them as well as teaching children on the visit. More will be said about different types of museums in Chapter 6 (p. 82). Some examples will be given here. In London, the British Museum welcomes young children and provides clip boards and pencils for study in a select number of rooms. Early history is the strength of the British Museum. The resources for the Archaeology in Britain Exhibition (1985–6) were particularly rich for schools. The disadvantage of this large type of museum is that the cases are locked and the objects cannot be handled. More practical is the Bethnal Green Museum of Childhood where children are allowed to handle toys which work, as well as look at the larger exhibits. In the same category is the Livesey Museum in South-East London where children dress up and use Victorian/Edwardian slates, rulers and pens and are taught by a Museum Education Officer in role play as a teacher. Different again are the Weald and Downland Open Air Museum at Singleton, West Sussex, a collection of medieval buildings on a large campus, the Beamish North of England Open Air Museum, near Durham, and the Jorvik Viking Centre in the crypt of York Minster.[32] All these experiences are breathtaking for young children and time must be given for them to look and look again without involving them in worksheets or answering questions on the spot. It is surprising what detail they will remember collectively if a quick follow-up is made on their return to the classroom.

The second 'must' for younger children is a visit to a stately home or other old building. I have already described my work with 6 year olds on our visit to Croxteth Hall, Liverpool elsewhere.[33] The National Trust owns many of these houses and usually provides more help for teachers than the properties owned privately. Very large mansions should be avoided as they are confusing to young children. Smaller houses such as Little Moreton Hall (Cheshire) and Haddon Hall (Derbyshire) are less formidable, especially if only one or two rooms are studied at a time. More houses are providing teaching rooms which can be booked where younger children can talk with the teacher and complete simple worksheets on firm tables or desks.

A third essential outside activity before the age of 9 is acquaintance with the near locality. Although more infant teachers are using the past in their work, Sylvia Collicott[34] seems to have caught just the right approach in her multi-ethnic school in Tottenham, North London. She took her infants for walks near the school to find shapes of buildings. Beforehand they studied shapes in school, drawing squares, triangles and circles and cutting them

out. The children took very clear photographs and drew sketches of the buildings on a frieze round the classroom. She says 'infants will quickly learn how to recognise a mansard roof on a Georgian building'.[35] Walking walls is another successful activity and small size children can see so much more of a town from the walls. Children can use plans and simple maps before they do the walk and/or when they return. There is the additional bonus of restricted space and therefore the need for good discipline for safety. Some schools visit Hadrian's Wall regularly, though this would be too much for children aged under 8, and only part of the wall near a suitable fort is advisable. There are many helpful books for teachers; a mine of information for all types of 'work outside' is *Look Around – Outside* by Henry Pluckrose (Heinemann Educational Books, 1984). Edpak is a new company which plans visits to historic towns for schools.[36]

Finding and recording information

Children should soon be weaned from thinking that their teacher is 'the fountain of knowledge'. Very gradually they should learn that there are many sources of 'finding out' even before they can use books for reading.[37] Pictures in books and on the wall, other children's pictures, slides, simple maps, old people and old objects are sources of information. Five to 6 year olds can learn to use historical words such as 'now', 'then', 'before', 'after', 'old', 'new' and to see them written down. Seven to 9 year olds learn about books from the contents page, index, list of pictures and flash cards of historical words to look for in books. In a storybook, such as those in the Ladybird series, they can put down the page references for one or two words such as 'battle', 'king' and 'castle'. All this is part of their normal language development.

A more sophisticated source of information is old documents. Five to 6 year olds in one school[38] used various primary sources to find out about their own local area. They first looked at a map of the local area and compared it with a map of the same region a century earlier. The children wrote creatively about the view from the playground as it might be one hundred years ago. They used the old map to find farms, lanes and footpaths, and the pictures from books about the Victorians to illustrate their work. They also brought into school old objects of the period and had walks in the area looking at the houses which were there in 1897, as listed by Kelly's Street Directory. The teacher read out the names of people who lived in their own houses in 1897 and comparisons were made between surnames and popular Christian names then and now. Census material provided the occupations of the local people which were very different from today. Obviously, the teacher had to work hard to provide understandable information from the primary sources, although 6 year olds love trying to decipher names on a big page.

Finding out from the right sources can encourage even very young children to record in their own special way. This recording starts with the teacher writing one word and then titles under pictures, the children doing the same and then progressing to phrases and sentences, using 'sentence makers' which should include historical vocabulary. They can also complete sequence lines and family trees (prepared by the teacher)[39] and would much enjoy reading an account of a visit, completing the gaps with words they should know. The missing words should be put on the blackboard at a first attempt. By 8 years old they should be writing short paragraphs about their work on the past. From the earliest years in infant school, children should keep their sugar paper Books of the Past[40] or history books[41] into which pictures, sequence lines, photographs and their own writing are fastened, to be kept by them all through the school. These books should be admired and talked about in the class and with the rest of the school and parents. Margaret Wallen, Dorset Co-ordinator for the National Writing

Project, emphasises the need for children to have an audience for their written work.[42] Thus displays of books of different classes at certain points of the year in the main entrance hall of the school are well worth encouraging. At Boutcher Church of England Primary School in Bermondsey, South London, all written work is done in draft which the children keep and after correction, write out neatly for display.[43] This system could be developed gradually from the age of 6 as soon as children are not dispirited by having to rewrite their work. Alison Prince tells of her 'shared authorship' with a class of 21 children of a book about how a London evacuee went to the Lincoln fens in 1939.[44]

Topics and projects

This chapter began by saying that all strategies depend upon sequence/time and topic. Sequence is a concept and topic a method of organisation or a timetable label. Before the late 1960s most subject areas were taught separately for a short time each week. History was usually taught chronologically through the four 'textbooks' of R. J. Unstead.[45] After the Plowden Report of 1967 teachers were encouraged to get children to find out for themselves rather than be told facts by the teacher. In 1978 the HMI survey, *Primary Education in England*, found that between 1967 and 1978 some teachers had acted upon the advice of the Plowden Report and others had retained subjects in compartments. The 1978 Report wanted some conformity and suggested more of a structured and planned approach. Efforts have since been made to retain the good features of the topic approach and incorporate more conscious planning into it.

Thus structure versus 'discovery learning' has become at times a controversial issue as far as topic is concerned since 1978. John Slater, quoted in Chapter 1 (pp. 1 and 3), has called topic 'a strange paradox undermining the unity of a discipline and presented as fragments of learning'.[46] Paul Noble in an amusing analogy compares the flow chart of a topic to an 'exploding spider' which blows up because there is no knowledge in it.[47] The enthusiasm of these experienced historians has to be tempered by educationalists who fear the return to the domination of the academic subject at the expense of child-centredness. Michael Bonnett[48] favours 'child-centredness as a source of structure' and gives seven questions teachers should ask themselves when planning topic work. The emphasis in all these questions is on the decisions and initiatives of the children themselves which apply especially to younger juniors. In the same edition of this journal, Colin Conner[49] favoured topic work 'balancing structure with freedom of choice for children', so that children can engage in 'discussion, argument and reflection'. The pragmatism of the teacher as to what 'will work', can be resourced and not involve too much preparation, is expressed by Peter Bell,[50] who favours choosing a topic which is biased towards one discipline and 'concentrates in developing appropriate skills and concepts'. There is much to be said for Peter Bell's approach.

In Appendix 6 of his excellent pamphlet Peter Bell suggests suitable topics for infants. He advises infant teachers to ensure that the five disciplines he writes about are included in a reasonable balance over the year. These topics might last two or three weeks only, according to the response of the children. Out of 40 topics, eight are historical ones (Ourselves, Robin Hood, Captain Cook, Guy Fawkes, the Museum, Homes, Early History and Clothes and Costume). Peter Bell gives detailed help on how to plan a topic, the importance of each child's topic book and the actual content of topics in 'Roman Times' and 'Life in the Middle Ages' for 7 to 9 year olds. Michael Hodges gives five criteria for history projects; a strong narrative line, problem-solving situations, potential for intellectually creative writing, mathematical concepts and care in the choice of topic.[51]

There are many recent examples of excellent topic work. Much of it is concerned with a local study of the area round the school but occasionally a special period of the past is undertaken. Alexandra Dilks[52] experimented with 33 7 to 9 year old children on Tudor history for a 16-week term. The children dressed their Cindy and Action Men dolls in Tudor costume, looked at slides and filmstrips of the period and listened to Elizabethan music. As the books the children found in libraries were too difficult, Alexandra Dilks wrote her own materials in short books for children to read on famous personalities. Groups of children made large books and models and also sewed their own Tudor costumes. After half term each child selected his own particular topic for a personal book which had to be neat and well illustrated. Christmas was celebrated by a Tudor banquet.

The second, more usual, type of project is well illustrated by the work of a whole school, a 5 to 9 first school, studying their own mining village: the reception class looked at 'old and new', the 6 to 7 year olds at farming, the 7 to 8 year olds looked at the village and its history and 8 year olds used documents, maps, old photographs and oral evidence to study the mining history of the village. A small group of older children studied their own school from log books and archive material as well as former pupils. These children had many difficulties in learning and the exhibition of their work for the whole village was a triumph.[53]

A very different village school at Sapperton, near Cirencester, has published the story of the village due to the initiative of their headmistress, Miss Pinnell.[54] All 26 children in the school were involved in this project covering 2,000 years of village history. Most types of primary evidence were used, in written form, in buildings and in museum visits. The activity of the children included role play, making bonfires, talking to visitors and above all making large, neat and beautifully illustrated books (Figure 5.11). This project had the ideal conditions of a small school in a good historical environment, an enthusiastic and able headmistress and much help from useful contacts. Michael Wood, of the BBC, also

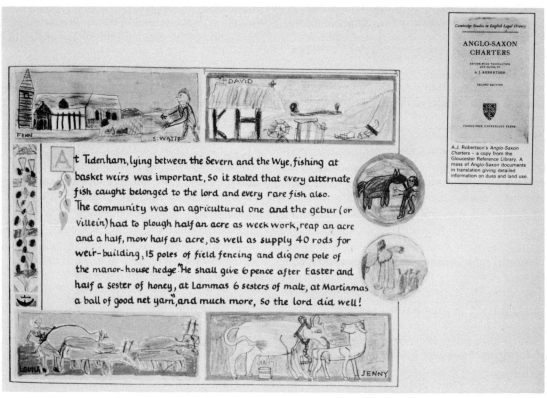

Figure 5.11 *A page from* Village Heritage *(Alan Sutton Publishing Limited)*

took a personal interest; in his Foreword he wrote 'the children of Sapperton have succeeded brilliantly in rooting out the main sources for the story of their village', 'this is a search which can be done for every place in the country'.[55]

In conclusion, let us look once more at Figure 5.1 (p. 51) which is a summary of this chapter. Although sequence and time are ongoing essentials of the teaching of history, they are usually most evident in an historically-based topic in the first school. Within the topic the variety of teaching techniques discussed in this chapter should be used. Few teachers will use them all, even in four years, and most will find which suits them best, taking the available resources into consideration. Teachers should look at Figure 5.1 as they plan the term or year's work in order to use as many techniques as possible to give variety to their work.

Notes

1. DES (1985) *History in the Primary and Secondary Years*, pp. 6–8. London: HMSO.
2. This teacher was helped by an excellent Teacher's Centre which she used well in advance. From here she was sent a large box on the Normans containing books, a filmstrip, artefacts and a wall display. She made worksheets for children to complete, used a film of the Norman Conquest and led a visit to the White Tower in the Tower of London.
3. DES (1985) op. cit., p. 4.
4. West, J. (1986) *Time Line*. Walton-on-Thames: Nelson.
5. See Chapter 1, Figure 1.3 for a horizontal time-line. A school decision should be made to adopt horizontal or vertical to avoid confusion for children as they progress through the school.
6. Northern Ireland Council for Educational Development (1984) *History: Guidelines for Primary Schools*, pp. 11–12. Stranmillis College, Belfast.
7. Blyth, J. E. (1982) *History in Primary Schools*, pp. 117–18. Maidenhead: McGraw-Hill.
8. DES (1985) op. cit., p. 5.

9. Blyth, J. E. (1982) op. cit., pp. 65–72.

10. Lally, J. and West, J. (1981) *Children's Awareness of the Past*, pp. 5–7. Hereford and Worcester: County Advisory Committee. See Chapter 3, p. 27 of this book.

11. Ingham, Jennie (1986) *Telling Tales Together*. Video and booklet from J. Ingham, The Cadmean Trust, 22 Newbury Road, Highams Park, London E4 9JH.

12. Collicott, S. (1982) 'Families are History', *Child Education*, May 1982; Ross, A. 'Children becoming historians: an oral history project in a primary school' (1986) *History and the Primary School Greater Manchester Primary Contact*, Special Issue No. 6.

13. See also Purkis, S. (1976) 'An Experiment in Family History with First Year Juniors', *Teaching History*, Vol. 4, No. 15; *Oral History in Schools*, Department of Sociology, University of Essex; (1987) *Thanks for the Memory* (How do we Know Series). London: Collins.

14. Jones, P. (1986) 'Primary Sources', *Times Educational Supplement*, 4 April 1986, p. 29.

15. Johnson, L. and O'Neill, C. (eds) (1984) *Dorothy Heathcote: Collected writings on education and drama*. London: Hutchinson.

16. Fines, J. and Verrier, R. (1974) *The Drama of History*. London: New University Education.

17. *Times Educational Supplement*, 4 July 1986, p. 8.

18. Wilson, V. and Woodhouse, J. (1986) 'Period Piece', *Times Educational Supplement*, 19 September 1986. See also Woodhouse, J. (1985) 'History through drama', *Child Education*, 3 April 1985.

19. Surkes, S. (1986) 'Stately homes – making a present of the past', *Times Educational Supplement*, 12 December 1986.

20. Harnett, C. (1951) *The Woolpack*, p. 22. London: Puffin.

21. Little, V. and John, T. (1986) *Historical Fiction in the Classroom*, TH59 Historical Association; Little, V. *et al.* (1986) 'Historical fiction and children's understanding of the past', *Education 3–13*, Vol. 14, No. 2.

22. Fidler, K. (1968) *The Boy with the Bronze Axe*. Edinburgh: Oliver & Boyd.

23. Treece, H. (1958) *The Children's Crusade*. London: The Bodley Head.

24. Welch, R. (1954) *Knight Crusader*. Oxford: Oxford University Press.

25. Low-Beer, A. (1986) 'Imagination and the use of historical fiction in school', Special Issue No. 6, *History and the Primary School*, pp. 22–5, *Greater Manchester Primary Contact*.

26. Unwin, R. (1981) 'The Visual Dimension in the Study and Teaching of History', TH49, Historical Association.

27. *And when did you last see your father?* by W. F. Yeames does not depict a particular historical occasion but rather a child's ordeal in an imaginary episode in the past.

28. Platts, J. (1968) *Activity Books*. London: Macmillan.

29. Blyth, J. E. (1984) 'Telling the Rest of the Class about our work on Croxteth Hall', p. 136 in *Place and Time with Children Five to Nine*. Beckenham: Croom Helm.

30. Blyth, J. E. (1982) op. cit., pp. 104–12; Newton, E. E. (1970) 'An Evertonian Spilling Over', *Teaching History*, Vol. 1, No. 4; Hart, T. (1971) *Fun with Historical Projects*. London: Kaye and Ward; Pluckrose, H. (1971) *Let's Use the Locality*. London: Mills & Boon; Fairley, J. (1967) *Activity Methods in History*. Walton-on-Thames: Nelson; Fairley, J. (1971) *Practical History Teaching*. London: Evans.

31. Davis, J. (1986) 'Artefacts in the Primary School', *Teaching History*, No. 45, June 1986 (for use with 10 to 11 year olds), Historical Association; see also Avon LEA (1983) *In Touch with the Past*. From Resources for Learning Development Unit, Bishop Road, Bishopston, Bristol BS7 8JS.

32. Pearson, G. (1985) 'Jorvik – inside the Museum Case', *Teaching History*, No. 41, February 1985, Historical Association.

33. Blyth, J. E. (1984) op. cit., pp. 125–42.

34. Collicott, S. (1979) 'Out and About', *Child Education*, July 1979.

35. Collicott, S. (1986) 'The Resourceful History Teacher, historical resources in the classroom', *Clio*, Vol. 6, No. 1, Spring 1986, ILEA.

36. Ed-pak, PO Box 42, Torquay, Devon TQ1 3JW.

37. Manley, D. (1985) *Information – Finding it and Using it. Help Your Child Series*. London: Hodder and Stoughton for W. H. Smith.

38. Avon LEA (1983) *In Search of the Past*, pp. 2–3, 4–5. From Resources for Learning Development Unit, Bishop Road, Bishopston, Bristol BS7 8LS.

39. Blyth, J. E. (1984) op. cit., pp. 67–71 for examples of sequence lines and family trees.

40. Blyth, J. E. (1978) 'Young Children and the Past', *Teaching History*, June 1978, No. 21; for more detail Blyth, J. E. (1977) *Young Children and the Past*. Dissertation for MA(Ed), University of Southampton.

41. Collicott, S. (1982) op. cit.

42. Wallen, M. (1986) 'First, find an audience', *Child Education*, November 1986.

43. Vulliamy, E. (1986) 'A school which breaks the mould in class', *Times Educational Supplement*, 10 November 1986.

44. Prince, A. (1987) *How's Business?* London: André Deutsch.

45. Unstead, R. J. (1950) *Looking at History*. London: A. & C. Black.

46. This came from a lecture by John Slater at a DES/History Advisers' Conference at Liverpool Institute of Higher Education, 16–19 September 1985.

47. Noble, P. (1986) 'History curriculum planning and exploding spiders', *History and the Primary School*, *Greater Manchester Primary Contact*, Special Issue No. 6.

48. Bonnett, M. (1986) 'Child-centredness, and the problem of structure in project work', *Cambridge Journal of Education*, Vol. 16, No. 1.

49. Conner, C. (1986) 'Children's learning and project work', *Cambridge Journal of Education.*

50. Bell, P. (1986) *History, Geography, Science, Nature and Religious Education Topics, Primary School – a Skills Approach.* Preston Curriculum Development Centre, Savick School, Ainsdale Drive, Ashton, Preston, Lancashire PR2 1TU.

51. Hodges, M. (1986) 'History projects for juniors', *Greater Manchester Primary Contact*, Special Issue No. 6, *History and the Primary School.*

52. Dilks, A. (1985) 'Time Travellers,' *Teaching History*, No. 43, October 1985, Historical Association.

53. DES (1985) op. cit., p. 8.

54. Miss Pinnell and the Children of Sapperton School (1986) *Village Heritage.* Gloucester: Alan Sutton.

55. Ibid., p. vi.

6 Resources for teachers and children

In a recent DES course on primary history, over 80 primary teachers answered a questionnaire. This showed that teachers were restricted to certain periods of history because they had few resources for other parts of the past. There is help from many sources for work on the Vikings, Romans, Normans, as for the twentieth century, the Victorians and the local environment, but little on other countries, most of the Middle Ages or British History 1500–1800. This shows that schemes of work depend upon resources and that teachers should avoid new courses inadequately resourced. In his analysis of the questionnaire answered by teachers, Peter Knight writes 'it is clear that history in school does not enjoy abundant resources'.[1]

The excellent project carried out at Sapperton School which dominated the school life of Miss Pinnell and her 26 children of all ages and abilities (see Chapter 5, pp. 71–2), used a multitude of resources. The buildings near at hand (school, church and stately home) were a very important concrete resource. One outstanding resource was the adults interviewed by the children; passers-by, the vicar, the pilot photographer, the archivist at Gloucester Record Office, the guard dressed as a Roman at the Corinium Museum, the curator of Stroud Museum, Lady Denny of Daneway House, two archaeologists, Moira Gobey, the school cook,

Mr Parker, a retired railway-man, and above all Michael Wood, the television presenter. Original historical documents and old books and maps were also consulted: the Victoria County History for Gloucestershire, maps of Sapperton in 1850 and 1910, aerial photographs, the 1851 census and the Bayeux Tapestry. The children also dressed up as Saxons, Stuart fighters and Victorian children. It would be difficult for any teacher to provide all these resources repeatedly for different topics and so many of them depend upon the particular environment of the school.

Most teachers would not have these advantages, but much can be done in more adverse circumstances if the necessity for historical resources is realised by teachers. History is too complex and broad a discipline to be catered for by one scheme of four books. The diversity of history and the need to show children different types of evidence means that each school must work out what resources it needs. Few are supplied by publishers, and therefore the teacher in charge of humanities must collect them gradually with help from colleagues, parents and friends of the school. The storage and administration of these resources should be near the staff-room rather than in one class store room.

Suggestions are made for the types of resources to build up in the flow chart – Resources for Teachers and Children (Figure

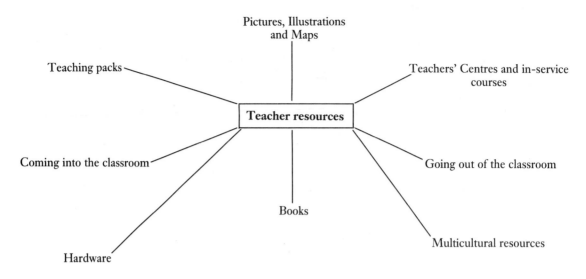

Figure 6.1 *Resources for teachers and children*

6.1). In a central position are the three essentials – the teacher, pictures and books. These are ever present resources kept in the store room. Almost as important are maps and diagrams, and 'hardware' which will not be specific to historical work but should be easily accessible on trolleys. Visits outside the classroom and inviting other people into the classroom are other means of obtaining resources. Teachers need their own resourcing through attendance at in-service courses, help from Teachers' Centres and from the reading of periodicals.

Teacher resources

At the beginning of the last chapter I wrote of the qualities needed by a teacher of history. One was basic knowledge of the topic taught[2] and the other was power of organisation. The latter is much needed in the collection and storing of resources. The general abilities of the teacher of young children and her experience are the most valuable resource of all. So much work in the 5 to 7 age range depends upon oral work that the teacher of this age range should be able to tell a good story, if possible without reading it, and to explain historical pictures and artefacts to the class as a whole. Her preparation of home-made posters, blackboard work and displays are the 'bread and butter' of the infant and junior classrooms. She also is the one to prepare large sugar paper books for each child or for groups of children and to compose 'gap' compositions, simple illustrated work cards and flash cards for children viewing slides or studying pictures.[3]

In my work on concept formation I prepared detailed questions on plain postcards to ask my children. I also spent many hours collecting suitable coloured postcards durable enough to stand up to handling by sticky or soiled hands. As I went around my six schools I found it necessary to wipe the postcards with a clean cloth ready for the next handling. In my test on the concept of power, I read contemporary accounts of the meeting in St Peter's Fields, Manchester from adult books, composed a simple version of the event, rewrote it after my pilot test and finally tape-recorded it to last only four minutes. This tape can now be used in many schools over and over again but its original preparation was time-consuming. If several teachers in one school could tape-record their favourite history stories (of about ten minutes each) children could use them in groups and colleagues could borrow them. There are many short history stories on world topics which could be read for tape-recording.[4]

During the last few years, children themselves have taken more responsibility in the organisation of the classroom. They have helped to write books and illustrated covers for publication.[5] Young children should be encouraged to make pictures, models, written accounts, historical friezes, large sequence/time-lines and family plans (trees) of famous local people of the past, for the school to keep as good examples of work and the teacher to use with the next class. Much display work is too often thrown away at the end of a topic when it could well be stored and retrieved as a starting point for new work another year. Teachers must not underrate what help their children's work can be to others.

Pictures and illustrations

Teachers and children make pictures by drawing, painting, using felt tip pens and collage work, and these items are usually personal representations of an historical character or event. They have their place in the teaching of the past, but artists' impressions and genuine contemporary pictures add an extra dimension to teaching and learning, although it is no easy matter to track these down and store them. Peter Knight has written of these problems.[6]

Large pictures for teaching history in the primary school were synonymous in the 1960s with the Macmillan Class Pictures, highly coloured depictions of conventionally important events in British history, with a touch of the 'John Bull' about them. The Pictorial Charts Educational Trust sells diagrammatic charts, charts combining diagrams and photographs, and pictures of people dressed in costume of different periods. These can be moved from room to room and are easy to store as they may be folded. I have used 'The

Medieval Village' with young children and found that it was clear, accurate and could easily be copied by children. Large pictures bought from museums often arrive in cardboard rolls and should be kept in them for protection. This applies to the long picture used in Chapter 5 of *The Encampment of the English Forces at Portsmouth*, showing the sinking of the *Mary Rose* in 1545 (see Chapter 5, p. 63), as it does also to the large pictures bought from the National Portrait Gallery (for example, *Richard III* and *Thomas More Family Group*) and the South Kensington Science Museum (for example, *Naval Shipbuilding in the Seventeenth Century*). The Tower of London has excellent prints of a *Longview of the River Thames* by Nicholas Holler in 1647 and a modern photograph of the Tower from the river. The journals *Child Education and Junior Projects* have large folded pictures in the middle of their monthly and bi-monthly issues. *History in a Nutshell* is a strip cartoon of British history useful as a constant poster in all classrooms to answer the question, What period are we doing this term?[7] The BBC publishes pictorial charts to accompany its programmes and an attractive Domesday Collection of very clear county maps is being published by Garnons Williams.[8]

Small pictures are more easily available in books, on slides or filmstrips (which can become large pictures if projected onto a wall or screen), as postcards, as photographs from the mid-nineteenth century onwards, on calendars, on tea towels or in packs of material (to be discussed later). Most teachers buy small sets of books instead of sets of 30 books; this enables children to find different types of illustrations for the topic studied. The *Looking at History* (A. & C. Black) series is good for outline figures to be traced or coloured but should be supplemented by *Focus on History* (Longman) in the coloured edition and *Living in the Past* (Blackwell), a more recent series. Obviously, children, even aged 6, should be encouraged to look for books in the public library with pictures in them and bring them to school for discussion. An attractive series, *The Camera as Witness* Macdonald, shows changing social customs from 1850 to the present in large photographs.

Slides are an easily stored resource enabling children to look at contemporary coloured pictures (such as medieval manuscripts), photographs of people and buildings and artefacts from museums. These can be bought from many sources such as museums, stately homes and normal slide and filmstrip publishers (for example, BP Educational Services and Longman). John Lally gives a list of the types of illustrations used by John West in his research.[9] During this work (1976–80) children individually used slide viewers and then came together in small groups to look at slides using a projector and small screen.

In one London school in which I worked, the teacher relied on postcards from museums and places of historical interest as visual aids; she found that they were small enough to be handled and tough enough not to be crumpled. She could also file them away neatly as they were all the same size. Her children spent a considerable amount of money buying postcards on their visit to the British Museum.

This also happened on a visit to the Tower of London with another school; there was such keenness to buy, that each child was limited to fifty pence for their purchases in the attractively set out shop. I relied heavily on my own coloured postcards for my sequence test.

Family photographs going back to pre-First World War and later are a treasured resource for teachers of young children. These are found in personal collections and in many recent books such as those in the *Into the Past* series by Sallie Purkis (Figure 6.2).[10]

Many calendars using fairly large pictures take an historical topic as a line of development such as banking, transport, costume and houses; these can form a frieze if put onto a roll of coloured paper.

I have also found tea towels convenient visual aids to carry easily without being crushed. I used a tea towel of the west front of Croxteth Hall, Liverpool, the Mary Rose and the Apprentice House at Quarry Bank Mill, Styal, with very young children most effectively. Tea towels have the advantage of being washable after sticky hands have fondled

Figure 6.2 *Two generations of the Guest family*

them! These are often sold in the shops attached to ancient buildings but similar ones can also be bought in ordinary stores. It is worth encouraging parents to buy an historical tea towel on holiday or on a family outing to encourage their child to find out about it and tell the rest of the class (Figure 6.3).

Another excellent genuine pictorial source is old maps and plans. These can usually be found in libraries, record offices and books. Some are large enough to act as visual aids for small groups. I have used the Braun map of Chester in 1580 to illustrate how I would teach picture reading in Chapter 5, p. 62 but most old towns have John Speed maps of 1610 for example, Southampton,[11] York and Chester. Bristol even has an old medieval map.[12] The plan of Lavenham in Suffolk in Chapter 4, p. 45, shows a medieval 'town' (village) clearly. County maps, as distinct from town insets by Speed and other cartographers may be too intricate for any but the 8 to 9 year olds, but if they are used it is advisable to obtain one showing the county in which your school is situated. Simpler than sixteenth-century maps are diagrammatic plans and dioramas of Roman towns found in museums;[13] the simple square pattern of very few streets enables children to make their own copies from the age of 7 onwards. This type of map enables young children to make a painless beginning to the essential skills of map reading.

Teaching packs

The archive teaching units of the 1970s, apart from those which were mainly pictorial, were too advanced for 5 to 9 year old children. One of them, *Some Kent Children*,[14] edited by Margaret Phillips of the Kent Record Office traces specific Kent children from 1594 to 1875. It is suitable for this age range because all documentation is supported by pictures

Figure 6.3 *Talking about the Mary Rose*

and photographs of children. More recent packs are slanted towards use with younger children. Teachers should keep their eyes on the *Times Educational Supplement, Teaching History* and newspapers for advertisements of new publications. One such comes from the Museum of Childhood, Lancaster. It is called *Children at Work* and is intended for use with a visit to the museum. Illustrated information sheets tell of the life of less privileged children at work in the factories and shops as apprentices and servants, and large black and white photographs give specific examples including children working in Third World countries today. One of the most appealing is the 'boy aged 8 dressed for shop work c. 1916' (Figure 6.4). The wealth of information attractively presented could form the basis for a whole topic on 'Children at Work Through the Ages'.

Also in the Lancaster area, this time the University of Lancaster, teachers of oral history will find help from *Voices from the Past,*

Figure 6.4 *A boy of 8 dressed for work, 1916*

1850–1940, which consists of four cassettes of working-class life in the North West of England, a set of 20 slides, a teacher's guide and copies of individual transcripts of the old people being interviewed.

Young children are intensely interested in archaeological finds and several new initiatives have taken place in the last few years to cater for this interest. An imaginative new initiative has come from the Department of Archaeology and Prehistory of the University of Sheffield. Professor Branigan and his colleagues have made up scholarly and practical packs for mainly secondary age children to use. Some of these, at very reasonable prices, are suitable for younger children. They are teaching packs of six broadsheets on 'Robin Hood' (history and legend), a pack of 24 slides of 'Gatcombe, the Excavation and Reconstruction of a Romano-British Villa Estate', and a pack of 27 slides showing what we can learn from human bones – 'Dead Men Tell Tales'. Kits available supply actual pieces of archaeological artefacts on a 'Roman Villa' and 'Animal Bones in Archaeology'. Full-size replicas of ancient tools and weapons on a 'Bronze Age Farm', 'Exploring the Roman Countryside' and 'Exploring Roman Towns' can be hired for two weeks.

Further initiatives come from the Esso Petroleum Company constructing a new oil pipeline from Fawley, near Southampton, to Seisdon, not far from Birmingham. This company had the foresight to finance the Trust for Wessex Archaeology in their digging enterprises. The result was that much was discovered about life between about 4000 BC to the eighteenth century.

The British Museum Education Service supplied excellent help to teachers and children for use with the recent exhibition *Archaeology in Britain – New Views of the Past.* A Teacher's Pack, and Children's Trails, a coloured poster and a video for loan and copying are excellent resources. Although most of the written material is more suitable for children aged 8 upwards, younger children could not fail to be enthralled by the discovery of Lindow Man in a bog in Cheshire and his reconstruction in Manchester Royal Infirmary. Young children in Manchester schools have been delighted by a drama group re-enacting the death of Pete Marsh, the Lindow Man, soon to be returned to the Manchester Museum. The Council for British Archaeology published a useful pamphlet, *Archaeology in the Primary School*[15] in which Shirley Echlin writes about her work in an infant school.

It is good to find commercial publishers beginning to provide more varied resources for young children and there are signs that more will fill this gap as the years go by. Philip and Tacey[16] have seized upon the idea of a *Clearview Activity Folder* in which each child keeps work cards. Sequencing is helped by a pack named *Self-Correcting Pictorial Sequencing* which gives the child the task of putting pictures of a story in the correct sequence and *Self-Correcting Picture and Text Sequencing* which adds text to the pictures. This activity could be developed by the teacher using pictures from postcards or her own work. Children could sequence a history story, previously read or told to them, from these pictures. Let us hope for more initiatives like this, developed into stories from the past.

Books

Textbooks should not be used, at least with infants, but small, well-illustrated topic books in large jumbo-style print and pictures from books written for older children are very helpful. So far few publishers have produced small books on historical topics and teachers have been thrown onto their own resources.

Few new titles have been published since 1984 when I made a detailed list,[17] although Macdonald have added to their valuable *Starter Series* a new volume called *My First Library* intended for 7 year olds upwards. Wayland have published the *How They Lived* series and Hodder and Stoughton, together with W. H. Smith, have produced an *Investigating Series* including two for history by Pamela Mays on *Towns and Villages* and *Roads, Canals and Railways*. Of those already in my previous list I still recommend the following publishers: Dinosaur (for example, *Castle Life*), A. & C. Black (for example, *People Around Us*), Usborne (for example, *Usborne First History*), Longman (for example, *Into the Past*) and Cambridge University Press (for example, *Activity Books*).

The 7 to 9 year olds are more easily catered for in the primary series produced by several publishers.[18] But some 7 to 8 year olds find the pages of such books too 'dense', the type too small and are therefore discouraged. Careful selection of historical fiction must be made for this age-group if they are to read and enjoy the books themselves. Examples of suitable books are David Rees' *The House That Moved*, a story about a Tudor house being moved at the decision of the city council, David Wiseman's *Thimbles*, a story about 11 year old Cathy finding the thimbles belonging to two very different girls who lived in 1819, and Clive King's *Stig of the Dump* about 8 year old Barney and his caveman friend, Stig.[19]

Teachers will find books intended by publishers for the 8 to 13 age-group helpful for their own preparation. An overall history of Britain is C. Wright's *A Children's History of Britain and Ireland*,[20] a well-illustrated and accurate volume. 1086 celebrations and the BBC Domesday Project have stimulated many books; the most suitable for our age-range for teacher preparation are Elizabeth Hallam's *The Domesday Project Book* and Nicholas Whines' *Domesday Then and Now* which traces an imaginary manor from 1086 to the present day (as Michael Wood did in his BBC programme).[21] For books on multicultural topics, teachers will find *Your World My World* by S. Shaw and M. Hawes (Scripture Union, 1985) and *Positive Books on Black People's History* (Primary Curriculum Development Project) of great value.

Peter Knight comments in his analysis of the Lancaster questionnaire that although the most popular series of books were the Oxford Junior History and those by R. J. Unstead,[22] these books cut across the general aim of teaching a 'source-based, concepts, skills and values approach' as the books are based on chronology.[23] Teachers on this course valued historical accuracy very little compared with the attractive appearance of the books.

Most schools make regular use of library loans when planning a particular topic, but if a television serial is being shown this often puts too much pressure on one historical subject. Library loans do not replace broad-based class and school libraries in which children can browse at will.

Going out of the classroom

This activity has already been discussed as a method of teaching in Chapter 5, pp. 67–8. It is also a most valuable resource and should be thoroughly exploited even with the youngest children. A visit is the first climax of any work, in the same way that the resulting display is a second climax of any topic.

In both warm and cold weather, museums are an excellent resource, especially those specifically prepared to help primary teachers. In Chapter 4 teachers were advised to base their scheme of work on what resources are available and this applies particularly to museum visits. The new Maritime Museum at Liverpool has published a pack on emigration from Liverpool to America in the nineteenth century; this is accompanied by five short cassettes which would help to broaden the outlook of children and lead to discussion about leaving home to live in a strange land. Dolls' houses of the last two hundred years are an obvious source of social history and can lead to replicas being made by the children in cardboard. Good examples are Queen Mary's dolls' houses exhibited at Windsor Castle, dolls' houses from 1690 onwards at the Rotunda Museum, Oxford and the many twentieth-century dolls' houses to be seen in general museums. National Trust houses and other stately homes are a resource in themselves and also sell pamphlets and packs to help children to observe in detail and to carry out tasks on their return to school. National

Trust Acorns are packs of cardboard rooms, furniture and figures which can be cut out and put together to show how families lived in another age. *Inside a Tudor House* is concerned with Thomas Stubbes, his wife Anne, two children and his servant Meg.[24]

During the last few years quite young children have been encouraged to use simple cameras to make their own pictures. Sylvia Collicott wrote of this in 'Out and About', Chapter 5, p. 69. In a novel article, Yvonne Davies describes the way she taught older juniors to use a video camera.[25] Therefore, one can at least advocate the use of a simple camera by 6 to 9 year olds. The creation of project books becomes so much more fun when children have planned and taken their own pictures of houses, castles, coaches and canal locks, to specify only a few examples. So the camera is a future resource of great value in 'going outside the classroom'.

Coming into the classroom

Going out on 'field work' has long been accepted as a praiseworthy learning activity. More recently people as sources of the past have been invited into the classroom regularly. This has already been discussed in Chapters 4 and 5 (pp. 36 and 68) in connection with family and oral history as well as in this chapter when discussing the Lancaster pack (p. 80). Teachers should particularly value old friends and relations of children, especially those over 70 years of age, as a vital resource. Their memories should be tape-recorded without delay. I was surprised when tape-recording the memories of a 92 year old lady how clear her memory was, how surprised she was at my interest in her life and how much she 'had lived in her own class', stating firmly that she had no views about poverty in an Edwardian city as she had never been involved with very poor people. The attitudes of older people are often restricted by the past and children should be aware of this.

As well as these older visitors, parents are

also welcome now in school and have been very useful in multicultural communities in telling children about the social customs and religious observations in other lands, (pp. 89–91). The National Trust Theatre Group tours schools acting appropriate plays and helping children with their role play and drama. With careful planning there seems no reason why this type of group should not be asked to write and act an historical play about Boadicea, Domesday Book, the murder of the Princes in the Tower or the death of Wat Tyler. A play which can be stopped for explanation and questions provides more learning opportunities than the watching of a film or TV programme straight through.

A final visitor as a resource is a 'writer in residence'. This phenomenon has become more customary in various types of educational institution. If the writer and children worked on an historical topic for half a term, there seems no reason why the writer should not help the children to write a book about their work, each group of children contributing a chapter, discussed and edited by the writer (see Chapter 5, p. 70). A professional writer could be a real help and relieve the teacher for other work or preparation of another term's topic.

Teachers' Centres and in-service courses

Resourcing historical work in the 5 to 9 age range is a slow task as there are no ready-made schemes published. The school has to decide upon a scheme which suits them (which should include a small or large multicultural element as appropriate) and then the teacher in charge of humanities has to build up resources. Although Teachers' Centres and in-service courses do not give sustained help, those which are provided are heavily over-subscribed and efforts are being made in many parts of the country to begin to satisfy this need. This mainly involves advice from lecturers and other teachers as well as publishers'

exhibitions. Those Teachers' Centres which are interested in this area of the curriculum usually provide very good resources for teachers, although at the time of writing they are slanted towards 8 to 11 year old children. Teachers then have to discard, adapt and add to them for 5 to 9 children. ILEA is an exception to this rule; a recent *Primary Newsletter*[26] is devoted to younger children with articles on 'A Victorian Home Corner' (instead of a Wendy House) and 'A Sylhelti Village Home Corner' (Bangladesh). As a result of an ongoing curriculum course run by Liverpool Education Authority, a group of infant headteachers have maintained contact with each other and formed a study group. The LEA grants certificates to teachers for attendance and adequate written work in history and geography in the primary curriculum.[27]

A more detailed and lengthy award is given by the Historical Association in its Advanced Certificate in the Teaching of History. This is taught by different academic institutions, mainly colleges of Higher Education, in various parts of the country and has outside moderators to maintain good standards. It caters for teachers of children in the 7 to 13 age range. At S. Martin's College, Lancaster, teachers are encouraged to base their assignments on experiments in their own schools. Those teachers I know have gained considerable stimulus for their work on the past from this Advanced Certificate.

The 1978 Primary School Survey encouraged, and subsequently the DES required, LEAs to consult teachers in their areas in order to publish guidelines, either on humanities in general, or history, geography and environmental studies separately. These are still being prepared owing to the pressure on teachers to change the curriculum in the last ten years. Some are published for all to buy,[28] but most of them are typed and only sent to local schools unless specific requests are made for them. Paul Noble analysed them in an excellent and honest article.[29] One-third of the LEAs (45) replied to the Historical Association request for guidelines; these were mainly concerned with content of schemes of work. Few gave very practical help to teachers on how to teach or what resources to use. Only two actually use the word 'history': *Teaching History in the Junior School* (Kingston-upon-Thames) and *Primary History 7–11* (East Sussex). The needs of 5 to 7 year olds are seldom discussed; Hereford and Worcester's *Geography and History 5–11* is an exception. Most of the guidelines are not confident enough to give detailed advice. Yet the fact that 45 LEAs have collected primary teachers together to discuss history in the curriculum and put their ideas onto paper is a step forward and a help to teachers all over the country.

Hardware

Many of the resources suggested both in this chapter and in Chapter 5 depend upon a television set, a slide projector, a photocopier and a cassette tape-recorder. Many primary schools now also have a microcomputer and a video-recorder. The availability of these can be a problem if they are in great demand. It is important for the school to check constantly that all machines are in working order otherwise frustration and delay will arise. 'Hardware' could also include models of buildings, dolls in costume and artefacts which might form part of a school museum, to be built up over the years and wisely insured.

I have found the photocopier an essential basic need for quickly providing class copies of pictures and written information without the enervating job of using a worn banda machine. Much published material can be copied for school use but copyright laws must be adhered to; the Education Office of an LEA or the Teachers' Centre should know the current rules about copyright. A slide/filmstrip projector is my next 'must' for showing children pictures and allowing them to view themselves, although one hopes that schools have small individual viewers by now. A film projector will not be used so frequently by teachers in a first school. A whole film is often too long for young children and there are few suitable historical ones. The North West Film Archives at Manchester Polytechnic have prepared seven teacher resource packs of contemporary black and white films on social life in the North West in the last hundred years. These packs may be borrowed; they consist of a silent videotape, text about the film, old photographs and audio cassettes of interviews with old people and those associated with the film. Some of the titles suitable for 5 to 9 year old children are *How Your Greatgrandparents Used to Live*, *Leisure and Holidays* and *Glimpses of Family Life*.[30] Although these films are about the North West, they are illustrative of the period as a whole and could be used in any school.

Third in order of importance is a tape-recorder, preferably six small models for group or individual work. Much has been said earlier about tape-recording memories and keeping them for future use. Children can also tape-record parents' and grandparents' memories at home and pool their resources in school. The teacher's guide book, *Voices of the Past*, gives specific help with interviewing (see p. 80). The teacher can also tape-record radio programmes which might be useful, or her own story-telling, or reading for her class to use if she is absent at any time. Children should be given a few lessons on recording techniques and the snags encountered with cassettes and recorders. Tape recorders, especially if battery run, should be checked regularly.

Television learning is a very popular form of activity in most primary schools. BBC, Granada and Yorkshire Television have made some excellent programmes, accompanied by notes for teachers and pupils. With the acquisition of video-recording machines by more schools, teachers are able to keep programmes and use them when they suit the school's scheme. Yorkshire Television publish a booklet, *Video News*,[31] describing all the videos sold by them. *How We Used to Live*, covering years from 1874 to 1953, may be bought, as may posters to accompany the series. The programmes are dramatised accounts of social life and are suitable for 7 to 9 year olds. *Passport to Treasure* is also suitable for this age range; stories of Quarry Bank Mill, Erddig, Lindisfarne, Snowshill Mann, Townend Farm and Cragside (all National Trust properties) are told in six programmes of 21 minutes each, with the help of an attendant ghost! Each one of these, if the children are well prepared, would be suitable for 6 to 9 year olds. *Family Album* and *Great Garden of Sleep* (graveyards) in the series *A Sense of the Past*, are 26 minute programmes, suitable as introductions to work on the two topics.

Two other programmes are even more popular with younger children. *Watch* (BBC) has the largest audience of any children's television series in the country. It is nearly always watched for the whole series and nearly always promotes a topic for the term. Most successful have been *The Egyptians, The Romans* and *Castles. Robin Hood* was not as historical and contained little help for beginner historians. *The Romans* (Summer 1986) was accompanied by a book for teachers which was well illustrated, practical and full of helpful information and stimulating questions. Such was the popularity of the programme that the British Museum published *The Romans Activity Book* to encourage schools to visit the Roman antiquities in the Museum. *Zigzag* is also a programme suitable for 7 to 9 year olds and featured a series on the *Normans*. Care has to be taken to plan a programme to fit into your scheme of work, especially now that video-recording allows greater flexibility. They should only be used as part of the school scheme and as an illumination, albeit outstanding, of the work as prepared by the teacher.

The microcomputer has become a popular piece of equipment in many schools.[32] John Sampson and students from S. Martin's College write:

THE COMPUTER AS AN AID TO USING EVIDENCE IN THE PRIMARY SCHOOL

There were 26 8 and 9 year olds of very mixed ability in my class of second year juniors. They were becoming used to discussion as a learning technique and usually worked as individuals or small groups in most areas of the curriculum. The school itself is situated on the edge of a large high-rise estate in Roehampton on the fringe of the ILEA area. The main shopping area of Roehampton centres around two streets that are mainly Victorian, though there are some more modern buildings, as well as one that possibly dates back to the Middle Ages. This little cluster of shops and houses is still called 'the Village' even though it is nearly surrounded by high-rise buildings.

The children had done some historical work previously when in earlier classes. This had been based mainly on stories, television programmes and the typical primary school history textbook. I wanted, therefore, to introduce enquiry-based learning and concepts, such as causation, change and empathy. I especially wanted to give the children the opportunity to use historical evidence, to make hypotheses based on this evidence and to test their hypotheses against other evidence. I hoped that a study of Victorian life based mainly around the local evidence would provide the framework for the children to become historians.

The children undertook a whole variety of work in the classroom, the village and the Victoria and Albert Museum. Initially, Trade Directories, a map of 1865 and the buildings themselves were the most popular sources of evidence for the children. We found the 1871 census returns interesting but quite difficult to use, especially when we wanted to collate and compare evidence. It was at this stage that we decided to create a data file for the census. We used the school's RML 480z and a program provided by the ILEA called SCAN. The children had some previous experience with data files by making small files about shapes and planets earlier in the year. After some initial discussion, fields were set up on the file to match the headings on the census return: schedule number, surname, forename, address, relationship (to the head of the family), sex, age in years, age in months (for infants less than 1 year old), marital status, occupation, birthplace (town) and birthplace (county or country). The extra fields were created so that people's presence in the Trade Directories of 1865 and 1888 could be recorded and therefore at a later stage compared with census information.

With some help the children entered much of the census material themselves. Soon groups were using the computer to discover a variety of interesting details and as a base for follow-up work. One group used the computer to compare the census return with the directories to discover that most of the traders seemed to have remained in Roehampton for some time, although some of the publicans seemed rather more transient! Another group tried to discover what children did in 1871; many worked at a young age, some were at school and some were not recorded as having any kind of occupation. A third group tried to discover why women were not normally recorded as the head of the household. Investigations into the data bank showed that only four women were recorded as head of the household. Basing their hypothesis on their own experience, the children decided that this was because the women were div-

orced or separated; they then referred back to the computerised data to check their hypothesis. An important lesson was learnt about Victorian family life and the use of evidence, when they discovered that in fact three of the four were widowed and the fourth was unmarried. A fourth activity was family reconstruction; the children enjoyed this and it helped them to differentiate between historical fact and legitimate hypothesis based on the evidence. To do this a number of children chose a particular family from the data file to write about. It was a great boost, of course, to be able to place a particular family in a particular real house, the exterior of which could be studied and sketched. Soon, however, the limit of the evidence provided by the data file became apparent; the details of family life were hard to find. Consequently, secondary sources were examined to find out about the likely furnishings, food, clothes and so on. Children increasingly justified their work by phrases such as 'the census tells me that . . .' or 'I don't know for certain but . . .'

Using the data bank had helped the children have easy access to, make hypotheses from and realise the inadequacies of a body of evidence and the way in which they could use secondary sources to support the evidence.

John Sampson, Roehampton Gate Primary School, London.

HISTORY 5 TO 9 AND THE MICROCOMPUTER

We have been working on a local history project with a class of 5–7 year olds using primary sources. We took them to a cottage which has been restored to mid-nineteenth-century conditions. Much of the follow-up work was based upon the BBC microcomputer.

One activity used a touch-sensitive pad called a concept keyboard. With the program PROMPT 3 we divided the keyboard into 16 areas (we could have chosen any number up to 128). Then, when an area was touched, the name of one of the cottage's features appeared

on the monitor. Drawings of the 16 features were laid over the appropriate sector of the keyboard. Now, touching the picture of the fire, for example, produced on the monitor the words 'fire, for heat and to cook on'. By adding words which they knew how to write, the children were quickly able to produce descriptions of their visit. FOLIO is a more sophisticated word-processing program which can be used similarly.

TOUCH EXPLORER also utilises the concept keyboard. We found it easy to program it with a plan of the main room. When touched, the name of the appropriate part came up on the screen. The children copied it onto a blank overlay and so reconstructed the plan. Having identified the room, the program was changed and the concept keyboard

Figure 6.5 *Lower juniors using the microcomputer and concept keyboard with a FOLIO word processing package*

was used to stimulate discussion about the cottage.

Later we used census data to focus on the people living in the area in 1881. With older children a powerful database program such as FIND or GRASS (which can produce graphs) or BETA BASE (which cannot) would have made it easy to study the whole population of 650. However, the infants needed a simpler program with a clearer screen display. FACTFILE and DURFACTS could have been used, but LISTS was preferred. The name, age, sex, job, birthplace and family size of 50 people, randomly chosen from the census, were put into the computer. Sampling, which has much to commend it, was necessary because LISTS could hold data on no more than 60 persons.

At first, in small, mixed-age and mixed-ability groups, the children browsed through the information. They then began searches, finding out how many children there were, what they did, and whether there were more males than females. Simple hypotheses followed, such as 'children did not go to school until they were quite old' and the children made searches to test them. In fact most of the three and four year olds were at school. What is more important is that the children found out something about the past themselves; that they were keen to find out more, and that they were keen to set up their own problems to pursue.

There are a number of programs which help make effective finished products. FRONT PAGE EXTRA allows newspaper-like work to be produced and FOLIO offers a good range of print faces and sizes. We had to use BIGPRINT which is limited in comparison. These programs are of value to any teacher wanting to make clear and bold work cards, story books and the like for children to use.

Had we the time, we would have used TRACKS to produce a simple simulation. Commercially produced history games and simulations are not generally suitable for infants, although the graphics from FLETCHER'S CASTLE are useful in showing how a motte and bailey was built. Lower juniors are little better served here.

Infants can make use of the microcomputer in their work on the past, and lower juniors, being better readers and writers, can do more sophisticated and more independent work. However, there are some difficulties to be aware of. The major problems are organisational, since only a few children at a time can work on the computer. Until the children are thoroughly familiar with the machine and with the programs, they will need frequent prompting. So, what will the other children do which is educationally worthwhile and which makes it possible for the teacher to be on call when difficulties arise? The limits on what young children can learn to do may be set by organisational factors as much as by their cognitive powers. Although we have not found any of the programs hard to use, they all have their own characteristics which it is best to recognise. It helps if children are taught about lists and ways of organising and searching them before they go on to learning how to use a database program such as LISTS. When using the concept keyboard with PROMPT 3 or FOLIO as an aid to word-processing, it is important to get the children to think about how best to draw upon the phrases it supplies for their own writing.

So, why should anyone try and use the micro with infants and face the sort of problems we have described? One answer is that the children are not frightened by the machine, that the technology has a motivating effect, and that sooner or later it is a technology which they will have to master. A second reply is that young children can say much more than they can write. The computer, using TOUCH EXPLORER or TRACKS can encourage discussion, and with the concept keyboard and appropriate program, it can help them to put some of that talk into words — words which can be edited and then printed and displayed as an attractive, finished product. A third answer emphasises the way the computer allows children to work with certain types of primary sources, doing real, investigative history from the beginning of their school career.

There are difficulties, particularly organisational difficulties, in using the micro-computer to help young children to find out about the past, but there are also advantages and rewards.

Programs

Many of these programs are available to schools at a low cost. Many LEAs have their own licensing and distribution arrangements, so it is wise to contact your LEA computer unit for advice on ordering.

Writing programs

BIGPRINT (1985) Barbara Maines, South House, Yatesbury, near Calne, SN11.
FOLIO (1986) Tediman Software, Southampton.
FRONT PAGE EXTRA (1985) MAPE III, Newman College, Birmingham B32 3NT.
PROMPT 3 (1986) Special Needs Software Centre, Manchester M13 0JA. (Also held by SEMERCs.)

Database programs

BETA BASE (1983) Clares Micro Supplies, Northwich CW9 7DA.
FACTFILE (1982) Cambridge University Press.
FIND (1986) Resource, Regional Centre, Exeter Road, Doncaster DN2 4PY.
GRASS (1985) Newman College, Birmingham B32 3NT.

LISTS (1984) Council for Educational Technology/SEMERCs.
OURFACTS (1985) MAPE III, Newman College, Birmingham B32 3NT.

Other programs

FLETCHER'S CASTLE (1984) Fernleaf Software, Gravesend DA11 0LH.
TOUCH EXPLORER (1986) Council for Educational Technology/SEMERCs.
TRACKS (1984) Council for Educational Technology.

Michelle Etchells and Elizabeth Heard, S. Martin's College, Lancaster

For some time primary teachers have been concerned to introduce multicultural resources into the classroom. This concern should be felt in all schools, whether or not their pupils come from ethnic minority groups.[33] Celia Burgess-Macey has been a primary teacher and advisory teacher for many years. Here she supplies a select list of useful resources.

MULTICULTURAL AND ANTI-RACIST RESOURCES IN THE PRIMARY SCHOOL

As teachers, we must first make ourselves aware of the biases that influence the writing of history books and expose children to an alternative perspective of historical events and people. In particular in this country most history has been written from the point of view of rulers and colonisers. An alternative perspective would need to look seriously at 'who' and 'what' is included, and 'who' and 'what' is excluded (for example, women, black people, the Irish, the working class). The following questions should now be asked. From whose point of view is the text written? Are other points of view included? Are people quoted directly or merely described by others?

I have tried to indicate where a text can be used directly by children, though in many cases they would need some adult help. I have labelled these 'A'. Books labelled 'C' are those which a child can read and understand for herself. I have divided the resources into the three sections of Britain, Africa and the Caribbean. I have omitted sections on Asia and America due to pressure of space. The sections do interrelate and an understanding of British history is not possible without an understanding of these other countries. In my view, to attempt to confine oneself to British history is in fact to fall into the racist practice we are anxious to avoid.

Britain

A Ali Arif (ed.) (1986) *Third World Impact*, Hansib. This gives photographs and documentary evidence of the impact and contribution of black people in twentieth-century Britain.

A 'Black Contribution Ignored' in *A Dragon's Teeth*, Short historical biographies, for example, D. Padmore, *Samuel Coleridge-Taylor*, Z. Alexander and A. Dewjee, *Mary Seacole, heroine of the Crimea* published by the National Campaign against Racism in Children's Books (1982–3) Nos. 13–18.

A Collicott, S. (1986) *Connections: Haringey's Local, National and World Links.* Haringey Community Information Service. This traces the links between Haringey and the world over 400 years with contemporary documents, engravings and photographs.

C Dewjee, A. and Alexander, Z. (1982)

Roots in Britain, An Exhibition. Brent Library Services. This is an excellent exhibition with clear explanatory text and illustrative material set out in sections, easily understood by junior children.

C File, N. and Power, C. (1981) *Black Settlers in Britain 1558–1958.* Heinemann. This is the most accessible introduction to the history of black people in Britain with many photographs, contemporary documents and evidence for children to examine.

A Institute of Race Relations (1985) *How Racism came to Britain.* A cartoon history which starts with the question as to why black people came to Britain and ends by explaining why racism came to Britain.

C Hasbudek, Zeynep and Simon, Brian (1986) *Zeynep – that really happened to me.* Altarf. An account in the words of a 7 year old girl of how her family fell victims to the Immigration Laws and their fight against deportation, supported by friends, teachers and commuity.

Africa

A Case, S. L. (1975) *Ancient Egypt.* Evans. Twenty-one topics of study on ancient Egyptian life with supporting pictorial evidence.

C Chijioke, F. A. (1983) *Ancient Africa.* Longman. This is a short introduction by an African historian to the history of pre-colonial Africa. It includes coloured drawings which make it more attractive to juniors.

C *Children under Apartheid* (1980) International Defence and Aid Fund. A photopack and book.

C Isichee, E. (1981) *Junior History of Nigeria.* Macmillan. This is written from an African perspective by one of Nigeria's leading historians. It is full of clearly presented historical evidence and illustrations. It is divided into 30 units, each covering a topic or period with suggestions for classroom activities.

C Murray, M. and Emecheta, R. (1981) *Our Own Freedom.* Sheba. Here are 90 photographs of women in Africa showing them in all aspects of their lives; farming, domestic work, childcare, market trade, wage labourer, career woman, in education. It is a very useful starter for discussion.

C Naidoo, B. (1985) *Journey to Jo'burg: a South African Story.* Longman. Also available on a cassette. This is a fictionalised 'true' story about two children setting off to find their mother who is working in Johannesburg. In their quest they encounter the harsh realities of apartheid.

C *A Picture History of Zimbabwe* (1983). Third World Books. A resource book for junior schools. Each page defines one word (for example, government, power, refugees) in the context of Zimbabwe's history. It has good black and white drawings.

A Sweetman, D. (1984) *Women Leaders in African History.* Heinemann. Lively portraits of 12 key figures in African history from Ancient Egypt to anti-colonial struggles.

C Timothy, B. *Kwame Nkrumah.* Longman.

The Caribbean

C Honychurch, L. (1979) *The Caribbean People*, Books 1 and 2. Nelson. Attractive layout and numerous photographs.

C Reid, V. S. (1979) *Sixty-Five.* Longman. This is an exciting presentation of the 1865 uprising in Jamaica in Marant Bay led by Deacon Paul Bogle, seen through the eyes of a young boy.

C Reid, V. S. (1982) *The Young Warriors.* Longman. This book deals with the Maroons, escaped slaves who set up free towns in the Jamaican Mountains and successfully fought off numerous attempts by the colonisers to recapture them. Two of the most famous were Cudjoe and his sister Nanny.

C Sinclair, H. *Toussaint L'Ouverture.* ILEA.

C Sinclair, H. *Marcus Garvey.* ILEA. Both these books are in the *Explore a Story* series.

C Thompson, B. (1976) *I Remember It Well.* Ginn. An autobiographical account of the way of life of a family living in a country district of Jamaica in the early twentieth century.

Celia Burgess-Macey, Haringey Reading and Language Development Team, Tottenham, London.[34]

Many of these resources are essential for the teaching and learning of history in the 5 to 9 age range. They are particularly useful as a 'way in' to discussion of the past with young children. Therefore it is necessary for one member of staff to be designated as a history (humanities) consultant, not only to initiate a scheme of work and help colleagues, but also as a person to be responsible for the collection, use and safe-keeping of resources in an easily accessible room. Until each school has a consultant, however enthusiastic teachers are to teach the past, no coherent and steady progress will be made.[35]

Notes

1. Knight, P. (1986) *Takeaway History*, p. iv. S. Martin's College of Education, Lancaster.

2. Books helpful to teachers are Nichol, J. (1981) *What is History?* Oxford: Blackwell; Macdonald, C. K. (1986) *Using Evidence.* Oxford: Blackwell; Jamieson, B. (1985) *History Detective.* Edinburgh: Oliver & Boyd.

3. Blyth, J. E. (1982) *History in Primary Schools.* Maidenhead: McGraw-Hill, for examples of work cards.

4. Saxey, F. (1960) *Classical Stories.* Oxford: Oxford University Press; Snelgrove, L. E. (1986) *Storyline History* (four volumes). Edinburgh: Oliver & Boyd.

5. *Village Heritage*, Chapter 5, pp. 71–2 of this book; Prince, A., Chapter 5, p. 70 of this book; Burgess, A. (ed.) (1986) *What did you do at school today?* Somerset Education Department, cover by Westfield Hant School, Yeovil; Wolverhampton Borough Council (1985) *The Time Tunnel*, work of children of Castlecroft JMI School, Wolverhampton.

6. Knight, P. (1986) op. cit., p. 103.

7. Smith, P. and M., 10 Tackleway, Hastings, East Sussex TN34 3DE.

8. Garnons Williams Publications, Hardwicke Stables, Hadnall, Shrewbury SY4 4AS. The largest size is 19″ × 14.5″.

9. Lally, J. and West, J. (1981) *The Child's Awareness of the Past: Teacher's Guide*, pp. 10–17. Hereford and Worcester: County History Advisory Committee.

10. Purkis, S. (1981) *Into the Past Series.* Harlow: Longman.

11. Blyth, J. E. (1982) op. cit., p. 77.

12. Low-Beer, A. and Blyth, J. E. (1983) *Teaching History to Younger Children*, p. 77, Figure 5, 1479 Map of Bristol, TH52 Historical Association.

13. Chester has a diorama of the Roman fort in the Grosvenor Museum.

14. Phillips, M. (ed.) (1972) *Some Kent Children 1594–1875.* Kent Record Office.

15. The Council for British Archaeology, 112 Kennington Road, London SE11 6RE. See also Wright, D. (1986) 'A Small Local Investigation', *History and the Primary School*, Greater Manchester Primary Contact, Special Issue No. 6.

16. Philip and Tacey, North Way, Andover, Hants SP10 5BA.

17. Blyth, J. E. (1984) *Place and Time with Children Five to Nine*, pp. 95–8. Beckenham: Croom Helm.

18. Middleton, H. (ed.) (1983) *Living in the Past.* Oxford: Blackwell; Mitchell, R. and Middleton, G. (1980) *History in Focus.* Harlow: Longman; Waplington, A. (ed.) (1983) *History Around You* (particularly *Starter Book* by D. Morrison). Edinburgh Oliver & Boyd.

19. Rees, D. (1978) *The House that Moved.* London: Young Puffin; Wiseman, D. (1982) *Thimbles.* London: Puffin; King, C. (1963) *Stig of the Dump.* London: Puffin.

20. Wright, C. (1986) *A Children's History of Britain and Ireland.* London: Kingfisher Books.

21. Hallam, E. (1986) *The Domesday Project Book.* London: Hodder and Stoughton for W.H. Smith; Whines, N. (1986) *Domesday then and now.* London: BBC Publications.

22. Burrell, R. *et al.* (1980) *Oxford Junior History.* Oxford: Oxford University Press. Also see p. 45, no. 73.

23. Knight, P. (1986) op. cit., p. v.

24. Saunders, B. (1985) *Inside a Tudor House.* London: Jonathan Cape/National Trust.

25. Davies, Y. (1986) 'Primary questions', *Times Educational Supplement*, 25 April 1986 mentions a Diploma course in Media Studies for primary teachers at Llay, Clwyd.

26. No. 19, Autumn 1986. History and Social Science Teachers Centre, 377 Clapham Road, London SW9 9BT.

27. For information contact Bruce Weston, Humanities Adviser, Education Offices, 14 Sir Thomas Street, Liverpool L1 6BJ.

28. ILEA (1980) *History in Primary Schools.* Centre for Learning Resources, Thackeray Road, London SW8 3TB; *Northern Ireland Council for Educational History*, Guidelines for Primary Schools, Chapter 5, p. 72 of this book.

29. Noble, P. (1985). See Chapter 4, p. 42 of this book.

30. North West Film Archive, Minshull House, 47–9 Chorlton Street, Manchester M1 3EU.

31. Non-Theatrical Programmes, Yorkshire Television, Leeds LS3 1JS.

32. Jones, R. (1982) 'Primary Schools, Humanities and Micro Electronics', *Teaching History* No. 33, June 1982 and *Microcomputers: Their Uses in the Primary School* from CET, 3 Devonshire Street, London; Sampson, J. (1986) 'Children as Historians: a Study of Local Victorian Families', *History and the Primary School*, Greater Manchester Primary Contact, Special Issue No. 6; Schenk, C. (1986) *Hands on: Hands off.* London: A. & C. Black.

33. Winkley, D. (1981) 'Multicultural policy and practice: a view from Grove Junior School', *Education 3–12*, Vol. 9, No. 1, Spring 1981; Antonouris, G. (1987) 'Multicultural Education at the Danesbury Junior School', *Primary Teaching Studies*, February 1987, Vol. 2, No. 2.

34. Primary Curriculum Development Project (1986) *Positive Books on Black People's History: for use in Primary Schools.* Aspen House, Christchurch Road, London SW2 3ES.

35. Campbell, R. J. (1985) *Developing the Primary School Curriculum*, pp. 78–9 for the role of the History Consultant. London: Holt, Rinehart and Winston.

7 Reviewing progress

We lack broad agreement about how to describe and scrutinise the primary curriculum. The absence of clarity and agreement about what children should be capable of at various stages of their primary education leads to a distinct lack of information about standards of pupil achievement in individual primary schools and a consequent difficulty of establishing any standards of achievement as a basis for an assessment of performance.

These are the words of Eric Bolton, Senior Chief HMI, at a conference in November 1985. Experienced primary teachers usually believe that they know the standard expected in each class in their own school in the basic subjects, but it is difficult for them to hold equally firm beliefs about specialised subject areas, especially those like history which often lack any recognisable pattern of progression. Most teachers would agree with Eric Bolton's argument that assessment is impossible without schemes of work for the whole school embodying the aims and objectives of the school. Therefore, good schemes and resources suitable for 5 to 9 year old children are the priority before assessment can take place. This has been discussed at length in Chapter 4.

Primary teachers are mentally assessing their pupils constantly and are in a better position to do this than their secondary colleagues as they see each child more continuously. Many of them feel that assessment of any kind smacks of the old 11+ examination, that it is an insidious attack on their carefully guarded autonomy and that completing record cards for each discipline is too time-consuming when word of mouth can pass information on in the staff-room. It is therefore necessary to justify such assessment and record keeping in history, to present teachers and children with clear objectives linked to age and to suggest efficient and quick ways of recording. A final objective is to involve parents in assessment by encouraging them to help their children and have an on-going involvement with teachers' assessments (see Chapter 6, pp. 79 and 82).

Objectives and progression in learning

Schemes of work should not repeat the same area of the past and should suggest historical topics within the competence of the child's age range. Family history is suitable with 6 year olds and the Victorians with 9 year olds, not vice versa, because younger children can relate more easily to their own family than those of a hundred years ago. Most experi-

Reference and information – finding skills	Can scan pictures and simple books. Can read simple accounts. Can use page references.
Skills in chronology	Can use basic vocabulary (e.g. 'now' – 'before'). Begins to understand the chronology of the year (e.g. seasons); and begins to record on a wall chart sequence of stories heard. Can put some historical pictures and objects in sequence.
Language and historical ideas	Can 'use' terms commonly used in stories of past (e.g. hero – queen – sheriff). Begins to use words such as 'the past', 'myth', 'true'.
Use and analysis of evidence	Can describe the main features of concrete evidence of the past (e.g. artefacts) and hypothesise as to their use. Is familiar with the question 'How do we know?'
Empathetic understanding	Can say, write or draw what they think it felt like in response to some historical story that has been heard.
Asking historical questions	Begins to become aware of basic historical questions, e.g. What happened and when? Why did it happen? How do we know?
Synthesis and communication using basic ideas	Using memory and recall, can describe orally and in writing some past events or story in narrative or dramatic form. Can make a pictorial representation.

Figure 6.6 *Some objectives for pupil progress in historical skills – by the age of 8 (from DES (1985)* History in the Primary and Secondary Years – an HMI View, *pp. 18–19)*

enced teachers know what will appeal to their class but it should be written into the scheme and adhered to for several years so as not to confuse colleagues teaching the same children in previous and future years. The recent DES pamphlet,[1] in a section called 'Progression and Pedagogy' gives in chart form the historical skills teachers should try to foster in children by the age of 8. This is indicated in Figure 6.6. Most of these skills have been discussed earlier in this book and methods of teaching to acquire them have been suggested. For example, my sequence cards on travel, houses, armour and costume helped towards 'skills in chronology'.

Concepts[2] are more difficult to understand by the age of 9 and the success of work designed to develop concepts will only be clearly shown later in the junior school. Yet concepts give meaning and purpose to any historical work and help children to group events and people in the past under different

'umbrellas' and so remember them more easily. The concept of similarity/difference is an essential one from the age of 5, closely followed by its expression through time as continuity/change. Development of these 'key concepts' should be started, using the knowledge children already have, such as the differences in children's height, weight, eye colour and hair colour. The children I studied found the differences between the two Midland Bank calendar pictures difficult to find, mainly because these pictures were not only different from each other but different from 'now'. Thus historical picture-reading for 6 year olds must include a contemporary picture; 9 year olds can cope with two pictures of other periods than the present. Studies led by Dennis Gunning and Jack Wilson at Trent Polytechnic advocate 'concept ladders' with the object of having only certain concepts in each age range to be worked for and built upon.[3] Change, sequence and evidence are the essential historical concepts for our age range.

The DES chart does not categorise 'attitudes' which teachers should want to inculcate. These are very long-standing aims affecting the whole of schooling, and unfortunately they are notoriously difficult to assess. The subject matter of history is particularly appropriate for developing 'morality'. So most parts of the past can lead to discussion of 'right', 'wrong', unselfishness and feeling for others. Was William of Normandy a tyrant in a foreign country or a good, strong ruler who united the English Kingdoms once and for all? Skills can be taught through practice but concepts and attitudes, particularly enthusiasm for the past, have to be 'caught' from the teacher.

Progression in learning is gained by more advanced subject matter and the building up of historical skills, concepts and attitudes. It is also helped by asking more difficult questions of children, expecting older children to answer the same question more fully, by setting more difficult written work to children involving longer answers and by marking (or commenting on) the written work more strictly. As children grow older they should be conscious of the need to present their work more neatly with fewer grammatical and spelling errors. One example of a simple and more advanced answer to the same questions might be:

Question : What do you know about the Norman Conquest?

Answer 1 : (age 7) William beat Harold at the Battle of Hastings.

Answer 2 : (age 9) William of Normandy wanted to be king of England instead of Harold. He prepared to come to England and crossed the Channel in boats full of soliders. After a long fight he killed Harold at Hastings and became king of England.

Such questions should figure in a systematic but practicable programme intended to keep track of children's development over the years.

Reviewing progress of the individual child

5 to 7 year olds

There are three ways of doing this and all methods should be used. One way is oral discussion with each child, as I was able to do in my 'one-to-one' testing of concepts. Class discussion can also show which children are especially enthusiastic about the past. 'The possibilities of structured and imaginative oral assessment are seldom exploited' are the words of the DES pamphlet.[4] This is an ongoing activity. A second way is for each child always to have a book he makes himself, connected with history; I called it a Book of the Past (see p. 73, Note 40) and Sylvia Collicott (p. 73, Note 12) calls it a History Book with straightforward candour. At the end of the year or when the last history topic has been studied, children should spend a special session looking at each other's books in their group and tape-recording their views for the teacher to replay. This would involve the teacher in listening to five or six tapes for the whole class. Although young children should not be encouraged simply to put the books in rank order of success, the teacher can usually gauge the point of view of the group. This method could be extended to group work on a frieze or collage. The third way, following on from the previous two, is for the teacher to make a final assessment once a year and put an 'H' on the normal record card to show an interest or capability in history. In the second of these two years more children should get an 'H' on their card and some may have two 'Hs'.

7 to 9 year olds

Four ways of approaching the assessment of this age-group are suggested. The first is oral discussion with each child and the class as a

HISTORY AND ME		
NAME		CLASS
How did your work turn out?		
What did you enjoy most about it?		
In what ways could your work be improved?		
How good are you at:	Your score 1 2 3	Say more here if you want to
1 Finding information from books		
2 Finding information from pictures		
3 Sequencing events and people		
4 Using the language of history		
5 Guessing answers from old objects		
6 Feeling like a person from the past		
7 Asking questions What? Why? How?		
8 Remembering the past		
9 Talking about the past with others		
10 Drawing a picture about the past		
11 Writing a story about the past		
12 Comparing people and events in the past		

Key
1 Good
2 Moderate
3 Not good

Figure 6.7 *Adapted from table used by College Heath Middle School, Mildenhall, by kind permission of Gordon Ewing*

HISTORY CLASS PROFILE

FIRST SCHOOL   1987–91

Aims and Objectives	Reception Class *Mrs Jones*	6–7 Years *Mr Forsyth*	7–8 Years *Miss Blake*	8–9 Years *Mrs Webster*
Knowledge of – Local history / History stories	No local. Stories based on Royal Family selections back to Henry VIII. Class frieze of royalty.	Visit to Tudor Museum. Stories about Tudor times e.g. Mary Rose, Mary Stuart.	No local. Stories of Vikings and Romans.	No local. Stories of Medieval history e.g. Roland of Roncesvalles – Burghers of Calais.
Understanding and use of historical language	Can understand 'now', 'then', 'yesterday', 'before', 'often', 'long ago'.	Extending language to 'century', 'court', 'progress'.	Started historical vocabulary books – all keen on this.	Finding many new words and using them correctly e.g. 'manor', 'serf', 'noble'.
Skills of evidence, reading, finding information and comparisons	Used artefacts of Edwardian school and compared with own school. Discussed history pictures and made their own.	Artefacts of the Mary Rose in pictures – understood and related to Tudor life. Writing one word titles and gap compositions.	Oral work with old people and taped them. Most children can write one paragraph on a topic. Not much reading done.	Not much evidence used but much reading done for projects, e.g. 'Focus' books from Longman – 'Living in the Past' (Blackwell).
Empathy	Not much.	Role play of Elizabeth I's Court began shakily but ¼ class showed talent.	Some discussion of points of view after stories of Boadicea and Alfred.	Difficult to empathise – beginning made with King John and Joan of Arc.
Sequence and Time Sense	Can sequence own lives on time-line and relate to 'before' and 'after'.	Simple Tudor family tree used for sequence in generations.	Most grasped sequence of events and a few dates, e.g. 400 AD.	Detailed class time-line for Norman Conquest – months and years used. Most grasped and made own.
Topic/Project/Centre of interest	Class frieze on royalty led to centre of interest on Our Families – parents and grandparents participated.	Topic of Tudor Times involved frieze, note-books, pictures, role-play, visit. Comparison of Royal Family and Tudor family, using last year's work.	Topic not undertaken.	Individual projects on themes in Medieval history, e.g. costume, chivalry, castles. Half class coped well. Very varied results but all tried.

Figure 6.8 *History class profile*

whole. For example, one would expect to have more Answer 2 type replies to the question about the Normans (see p. 95). In my research I did not find that older children were more articulate or relevant in oral work than infants. By this stage the second way of assessing at the end of the year could take the form of each child completing a simple schedule, as in Figure 6.7. The schedule should be explained to the class as a whole, each child having a copy on his table, and children should be encouraged to be honest and not be expected to complete all sections. The third form of assessment, of individual books or collective work on frieze or collage, should be done in groups. The discussions in groups should be tape-recorded for the teacher's use. The last form is the teacher using all the other methods to complete record cards. These should have a space for history, geography, social studies/humanities or topic, according to school policy. In this space the teacher should put 'H_1', 'H_2' or 'H_3'. Care should be taken not to underestimate individual schedules which show humility rather than arrogance.

Reviewing progress of the class: history class profile

Both individual and class assessment are ideal as methods of review, but some teachers may not have time to do both. In that case the class profile is the most helpful, as it should include information for the next class teacher to use. Figure 6.8 is a suggestion covering the years 5 to 9, thus in many cases straddling two schools. This is an imaginary class profile using practicable (if optimistic) schemes of work as a basis. Broadly speaking, the content of history for this imaginary school is family history (5–6), the Tudors (6–7), the Vikings and Romans (7–8) and the Middle Ages (8–9). It should be clear to the four teachers concerned that a large time-line from 1000 BC to the present day is needed to place the periods

studied in relation to each other. There is no chronological syllabus involved. This profile goes up the school with the class and is completed in this straightforward fashion by each class teacher. It could be photocopied and given to the next school the children attend. Together with the letter 'H' on the individual record of each child, and the child's own assessment, this profile should provide good information for use in the present or future school. Glancing at the profile any teacher could soon find out what types of activity had been omitted or overemphasised in previous years. This would not render the history schemes unnecessary as all teachers would be basing the profile on it.

Accountability may have loomed too large in recent discussions and we must be careful not to return to 'payment by results' of the later nineteenth century. If teaching is good, assessment can be easy and need not be time consuming. It will be the wish of teachers, children and parents to facilitate assesment and learn from it. As *The Curriculum 5–16*[5] agrees it is 'inseparable from the teaching process' and should improve children's learning and help teachers to improve the curriculum and their teaching techniques.

Notes

1. DES (1985) *History in the Primary and Secondary Years – An HMI View*. London: HMSO.
2. Elliott, G. (1976) *Teaching for Concepts*. School Curriculum Development Committee.
3. Wilson, J. (1984) 'Quality and progression in primary school topic work using concept ladders', *Concept Ladders in Primary School Topic Work*. Trent Papers in Education, Trent Polytechnic, Nottingham.
4. DES (1985) op. cit., p. 20.
5. DES (1985) *The Curriculum 5–16: Curriculum Matters 2*. An HMI Series, p. 51 as quoted by Colin Richards. London: HMSO; (1986) 'The curriculum from 5 to 16: background, content and some implications for primary education', *Greater Manchester Primary Contact*, Vol. 4, No. 1, pp. 27–36.

Appendix 1: Useful addresses

Archaeology in Education, Department of Archaeology and Prehistory, University of Sheffield, Sheffield S10 2TN.

Association of Teachers of Family History, c/o Thomas Nelson and Sons, Nelson House, Mayfield Road, Walton-on-Thames, Surrey KT12 5PL.

Avon Resources, Resources for Learning Development Unit, Bishops Road, Bishopston, Bristol BS7 8LS.

Cambridge Journal of Education, Institute of Education, Shaftesbury Road, Cambridge CB2 2BX.

Centre for North West Regional Studies, University of Lancaster, Bailrigg, Lancaster.

Child Education and *Junior Education*, Scholastic Publications Ltd, Westfield Road, Leamington Spa, Warwickshire CV33 0JH.

The Council for British Archaeology, 112 Kennington Road, London WC1B 3QQ.

The Cranborne Chase and Dorset Projects for 5 to 9 Schools, c/o Joan Hickmott, Primary Adviser, County Hall, Dorchester, Dorset DT1 1XJ.

English Heritage, Education Service, 15/17 Great Marlborough Street, London W1V 1AF.

Esso Petroleum Co. Ltd, Corporate Affairs Department, Esso UK, Esso House, Victoria Street, London SW1E 5JW.

Essex Curriculum Extension Project, Threadneedle Street, Market Road, Chelmsford, Essex CM1 1LD.

Garnons Williams Publications, Hardwicke Stables, Hadnall, Shrewsbury, Shropshire SY4 4AS (Domesday Maps).

Greater Manchester Primary Contact, Didsbury School of Education, Manchester Polytechnic, 799 Wilmslow Road, Manchester M20 8RR.

Group for Education in Museums, 389 Great Western Road, Aberdeen AB1 6NY.

Heritage Education Trust, St Mary's College, Strawberry Hill, Twickenham TW1 4SX.

Historical Association, 59A Kennington Park Road, London SW11 4JH. (*Teaching History* is the journal of the Historical Association.)

ILEA Centre for Learning Resources, Thackeray Road, London SW8 3TB.

ILEA History and Social Sciences Teachers' Centre, 377 Clapham Road, London SW9 9BT.

Lancashire Museum Education Service, Judges' Lodgings, Museum of Childhood, Church Street, Lancaster LA1 1YS.

The National Trust, PO Box 30, Beckenham, Kent BR3 4TZ.

North West Film Archive, Minshull House, 47–9 Chorlton Street, Manchester M1 3EU.

Philip and Tacey, Northway, Andover, Hertfordshire SP10 5BA.

Pictorical Charts Educational Trust, 23 Kirchen Road, West Ealing, London W13 0UD.

Primary Curriculum Development Project, Aspen House, Christchurch Road, London SW2 3ES.

Primary Teaching Studies, Department of Teaching Studies, Polytechnic of North London, Prince of Wales Road, London NW5 3LB.

School Curriculum Development Committee, Newcombe House, 45 Notting Hill Gate, London W11 3JB.

School in the World, World Development Centre, St Katherine's College, Strand Park Road, Liverpool L16 9JD.

Teachers' Centre, Queens University, Belfast, Upper Crescent, University Road, Belfast BT7 1NT.

Tower of London, Department of Environment, 25 Savile Row, London W1X 2BJ.

Treasure Chest for Teachers, Teacher Publishing Co. Ltd, Derbyshire House, Lower Street, Kettering, Northamptonshire NN16 8BB.

Appendix 2: Museums and historic houses referred to

Althorp House, Northampton (for parties and special times or booking write, enclosing sae, to The Countess Spencer, Althorp, Northampton NN7).

Beamish North of England Open Air Museum, nr Chester-le-Street, Co. Durham (tel: 0207 231 811).

Bethnal Green Museum of Childhood, Cambridge Heath Road, London E2 9PA (tel: 01 980 2415).

Bristol City Museum and Art Gallery, Queen's Road, Bristol BS8 1RL (tel: 0272 299 771).

British Museum, Great Russell Street, London WC1B 3DG (tel: 01 636 1555).

Castle Hill, 19th Century Cottage Museum, Lancaster (tel: City Museum, 0524 64637).

Clarke Hall Educational Museum, Aberford Road, Wakefield, Yorkshire (tel: 0924 375 598).

Croxteth Hall and Country Park, Liverpool (tel: 051 228 5311).

Fitzwilliam Museum, Trumpington Street, Cambridge CB2 1RB (tel: 0223 69501).

Gallery of English Costume, Platt Hall, Platt Fields, Rusholme, Manchester (tel: 061 224 5217).

Geffrye Museum, Kingsland Road, Shoreditch, London E2 8EA (tel: 01 739 8368).

Haddon Hall, Bakewell, Derbyshire (tel: 062 981 2855).

Hardwick Hall, nr Chesterfield, Derbyshire (tel: 0246 850 430).

Jorvik Viking Centre, Coppergate, York (tel: 0904 643 211).

Kentwell Hall, Long Melford, Suffolk.

Lancaster City Museum, Market Square, Lancaster (tel: 0524 64637).

Little Moreton Hall, Congleton, Cheshire CW12 4SD (tel: 0260 272 018).

Livesy Museum, 682 Old Kent Road, London SE15 1JR (tel: 01 639 5604).

Maritime Museum, Mann Island, Pier L3, Liverpool (tel: 051 236 5567).

Museum of History of Education, University of Leeds (tel: 0532 431 751).

Rotunda Museum of Antique Dolls' Houses, Grove House, Iffley Road, Oxford.

Speke Hall, Liverpool (tel: 051 427 7231).

Sudbury Hall, nr Derby (tel: 028 378 305).

Tower of London, Tower Hill, London EC3N 4AB (tel: 01 709 0765).

Weald and Downland Open Air Museum, Singleton, Chichester, Sussex PO18 0EU (tel: 0243 63 348).

Windsor Castle, Windsor (tel: 0753 868 286).

Select Bibliography

General

DES (1982) *Education 5 to 9: An Illustrative Survey of 80 First Schools*. London: HMSO.

DES (1985) *History in the Primary and Secondary Years – An HMI View*. London: HMSO.

DONALDSON, M. (1978) *Children's Minds*. London: Fontana.

ELLIOTT, G. (1976) *Teaching for Concepts*. School Curriculum Development Committee.

HEEKS, P. (1981) *Choosing and Using Books in the First School*. London: Macmillan.

TOUGH, J. (1976) *Listening to Children Talking*. London: Ward Lock.

TOUGH, J. (1977) *Talking and Learning*. London: Ward Lock.

General – history

AVON LEA (1982) *History and Geography in Primary Schools*. Avon LEA.

BLYTH, J. E. (1982) *History in Primary Schools*. Maidenhead: McGraw-Hill. (New edition expected 1988 from Open University Press.)

BLYTH, J. E. (1984) *Place and Time with Children Five to Nine*. Beckenham: Croom Helm.

FACULTY OF COMMUNITY STUDIES AND EDUCATION (1986) *History and the Primary School*, Special Issue No. 6 of *Greater Manchester Primary Contact*, Didsbury School of Education, Manchester.

ILEA (1980) *History in the Primary School: Curriculum Guidelines*. London: Inner London Education Authority.

JAMIESON, B. (1985) *History Detective*. Edinburgh: Oliver & Boyd.

LOW-BEER, A. and BLYTH, J. E. (1983) *Teaching History to Younger Children*, TH52, Historical Association.

MACDONALD, C. K. (1986) *Using Evidence*. Oxford: Blackwell.

MAYS, P. (1974) *Why Teach History?* London: University of London Press.

MAYS, P. (1985) *Teaching Children through the Environment*. London: Hodder and Stoughton.

NICHOL, J. (1981) *What is History?* Oxford: Blackwell.

NOBLE, P. (1986) *Understanding History*. Help your Child series. London: Hodder and Stoughton for W. H. Smith.

NORTHERN IRELAND COUNCIL FOR EDUCATIONAL DEVELOPMENT (1984) *History: Guidelines for the Primary School*.

History schemes of work

FAIRLEY, J. (1970) *Patch History and Creativity*. Harlow: Longman.

NOBLE, P. (1985) **Curriculum Planning in Primary History**, TH57, Historical Association.

POLLARD, M. (1973) *History for Juniors*. London: Evans.

WRIGHT, C. (1986) *A Children's History of Britain and Ireland*. London: Kingfisher Books.

History outside the classroom

FAIRLEY, J. (1977) *History Teaching through Museums*. Harlow: Longman.

JOHNSON, R. J. and IKIN, K. J. (1974) *History Fieldwork.*. Basingstoke: Macmillan.

LINDLEY, K. (1972) *Graves and Graveyards. Local Search Series.* London: Routledge and Kegan Paul.

PLUCKROSE, H. (1984) *Look Around – Outside.* London: Heinemann.

TITLEY, P. (1971) *Discovering Local History.* Kettering: Allman & Sons.

WEST, J. (1966) *History, Here and Now.* Kettering: Teacher Publishing Company.

Model-making and history

FAIRLEY, J. (1967) *Activity Methods in History.* Walton-on-Thames: Nelson.

HART, T. (1973) *Fun with Historical Projects.* London: Kaye and Ward.

Acknowledgments

The author and publishers would like to thank the following for permission to use material in this book:

Sallie Purkis, Jayne Woodhouse, Elizabeth Heard, Michelle Etchells, Peter Knight, Viv Wilson, John Sampson, Hilary Cooper, Gill Aslett, Celia Burgess-Macey, Elizabeth Bouchier, John Davis, Dr Colin Conner and Mr Ron Stewart for their contributions; Camera Press for the photograph on p. 4; Paul Noble for Figure 1.2 on p. 5; Essex Education Committee for Figures 2.4, 2.5 and 2.6 on pp. 16 and 17; The Avon Resources for Learning Development Unit for the photograph on p. 18; Sue Perrin for Figure 2.8 on p. 19; Mr Justin Todd for the two paintings reproduced on p. 23 and p. 24 which were commissioned by Midland Bank plc for the Midland Bank Group Calendar, 1971; City of Manchester Central Library for the print on p. 26; Liverpool Education Committee for Figure 3.4 on p. 29; Derbyshire Museum Service for the photograph on p. 34; BBC Hulton Picture Library for the photograph on p. 35 which was used in *Camera as Witness – Holidays* by Penny Marshall, published by Macdonald; The Fitzwilliam Museum, Cambridge for the photograph on p. 36; the town of Bayeux / Centre Guillaume le Conquerant for the illustration from the Bayeux Tapestry on p. 43; the Lavenham Publicity Group, Lavenham, Suffolk for the plan on p. 45; Thomas Nelson and Sons Ltd for the extract from *The Stoners* by P. J. Jefferies on p. 39 and the card 'Then and Now' from *Time Line* by J. West on p. 52; Chester City Council for the photograph on p. 53 and the print on p. 62; Tom Holder for the photograph on p. 59; the Portsmouth City Museums for the print on p. 63; Simon Wingfield Digby for the print on p. 63; The Walker Art Gallery for the print on p. 64; Alan Blyth and the Wirral Education Committee for the photographs on pp. 66, 67 and 79; Alan Sutton Publishing Limited for the page from *Village Heritage* on p. 72; the Documentary Photography Archive for the photograph on p. 80; Peter Knight for the photograph on p. 87; the Controller of Her Majesty's Stationery Office for the table on p. 94 and Gordon Ewing for Figure 6.7 on p. 96. Peter Knight would also like to thank Mr M. Croft, Mrs V. Pearson and Mrs M. Waite who made it possible for him to write his contribution. The cover photo is by Sally and Richard Greenhill.

Index

Pinnell, Miss 71, 75
Plowden Report 1, 7, 70
posters 76, 84
prehistoric 43
progression 50, 95
psychologists 8, 28, 30
Purkis, S. 33, 40, 41, 78

Quarry Bank Mill (Styal) 78, 85

recording 47, 51, 69, 70
record card 95
role-play 11, 27, 28, 57–61, 62, 65, 68, 83, 97
Romans 2, 4, 11, 35, 51, 67, 71, 79, 80, 85, 97
Royalty 3, 37, 38, 97

Sampson, J. 85–6
Sapperton 71–2, 75
Schools Council Working Paper 48, 57
Schools television *see* television
sequence *see* time
Slater, J. 1, 2, 3, 6, 7, 70
slides 65, 78, 80
  slide-projector 84
  slide viewer 65, 78
social studies 41, 50, 98
spiral curriculum 8
story-telling 13, 19, 20, 25, 26, 40, 46, 47, 48, 53,
    54, 56, 57, 58, 67, 76, 77, 84, 88
  Telling Tales Together 55

talking 26, 27, 51, 54
tape-recording 40, 54, 55, 65, 66, 76, 82, 84, 95, 98
teachers' centres 57, 76, 83–4
teaching packs 79–81

television 3, 5, 25, 26, 42, 82, 84, 85
Third World 41, 80
Thompson, F. 15, 16
time/sequence 2, 6, 11, 12, 13, 17, 18, 19, 25, 27,
    28, 30, 33, 44, 51, 53, 54, 61, 65, 94, 97
  time-line 6, 11, 32, 36, 37, 38, 42, 43, 56, 57, 66,
    70, 98
Times Educational Supplement 58, 80
topic 47, 51, 70–2
trade directories 85–6
triangulation 20
Tower of London 30, 44, 77, 78
Tudor 30, 36, 44, 51, 58, 62, 63, 64, 71, 81, 82, 97

Universities
  Essex 40
  Kent 40
  Lancaster 80
  Leicester 20
  Sheffield 80
Unwin, R. 61, 70

Victorians 6, 18, 19, 28, 34, 36, 43, 51, 69, 70, 85,
    86, 93
video-record 42, 84, 85
visits 8

West, J. 1, 5, 7, 8, 13, 53, 54, 78
William of Normandy 44, 51, 58, 95
Wood, M. 71, 75, 81
Woodhouse, J. 58–60
work cards 76
World Wars 4, 33, 38, 41, 64, 67, 78
writing 29, 33, 40, 67, 71, 83, 97